CW00407028

THE EURO♡ISION

SONG CONTEST

THE OFFICIAL CELEBRATION

The publishers would like to thank the following sources for their kind permission to reproduce the pictures in this book.

Key: t=Top, b=Bottom, m=Middle, l=Left and r=Right

Page 5 Hulton Archive/Getty Images; 6 John Kennedy O'Connor; 7 Redferns/Getty Images; 8-9 Jonathan Nackstrand/Getty Images; 10t Mondadori/Getty Images; 10b Mondadori/Getty Images; 11t John Kennedy O'Connor; 11m John Kennedy O'Connor; 11b John Kennedy O'Connor; 12t David Redfern/Getty Images; 12b John Kennedy O'Connor; 13t John Kennedy O'Connor; 13b Andrew Putler/Getty Images; 14t John Kennedy O'Connor; 14b Times Newspapers/Rex Features; 15 John Kennedy O'Connor; 16l John Kennedy O'Connor; 16r Wilkinson/Daily Mail/Rex Features; 17t Sipa Press/Rex Features; 17b Keystone/Getty Images; 18 Rex Features; 19t Pat Maxwell/Rex Features; 19m John Kennedy O'Connor; 19b Rolls Press/Popperfoto/Getty Images; 20 Popperfoto/Getty Images; 21t Lehtikuva/Rex Features; 21b John Kennedy O'Connor; 22 Ted Black/Rex Features; 23t Sean Gallup/Getty Images; 23b Derek Cattani/Rex Features; 24t Daily Sketch/Rex Features; 24b Pat Maxwell/Rex Features; 25l John Kennedy O'Connor; 25r AFP/Getty Images; 26t Keystone/Getty Images; 26m John Kennedy O'Connor; 26b Sean Gallup/Getty Images; 27 John Kennedy O'Connor; 28l Alinari/Rex Features; 28r John Kennedy O'Connor; 29 Keystone/Getty Images; 30 Frank Barratt/Getty Images; 31l Popperfoto/Getty Images; 31r John Kennedy O'Connor; 32t East News/Rex Features; 32b AFP/Getty Images; 33t John Kennedy O'Connor; 33b Pablo Blazquez Dominguez/Getty Images; 34 AP/Topfoto; 35t John Kennedy O'Connor; 35b Ragnar Singsaas/Rex Features; 36t Sean Gallup/Getty Images; 36b Rex Features; 37 Derek Cattani/Rex Features; 38-39 Pat Maxwell/Rex Features; 40 Sten Rosenlund/Rex Features; 42 Mustafa/Getty Images; 43 Janek Skarzynski/Getty Images; 44l Jorgen Angel/Getty Images; 44r Rolf Klatt/Rex Features; 45t Michael Ochs Archives/Getty Images; 45b Patrick Piel/Getty Images; 46 Pekka Sakki/Rex Features; 47 John Kennedy O'Connor; 48-49 AFP/Getty Images; 50 ITV/Rex Features; 51 Rex Features; 52 Birger Vogelius/Rex Features; 53 Sergei Supinsky/Getty Images; 54l Action Press/Rex Features; 54r Pat Maxwell/Rex Features; 55 Rolf Klatt/Rex Features; 56l Lehtikuva/Rex Features; 56r John Kennedy O'Connor; 57t Rex Features; 57b Action Press/Rex Features; 58t Mick Hutson/Getty Images; 58b John Kennedy O'Connor; 59 Ragnar Singsaas/Getty Images; 60t Pat Maxwell/Rex Features; 60-61b IBL/Rex Features; 61t Associated Newspapers/Rex Features; 62 Sten Rosenlund/Rex Features; 63 Janek Skarzynski/Getty Images; 64-65 Rolf Klatt/Rex Features; 65 Chris Capstick/Rex Features; 66l John Kennedy O'Connor; 66r Action Press/Rex Features; 68 AFP/Getty Images; 69t Jonathan Nackstrand/Getty Images; 69b Anadolu Agency/Getty Images; 70 Keystone/Getty Images; 71 Gianni Ferrari/Getty Images; 72 John Kennedy O'Connor; 73 Lehtikuva/Rex Features; 74 Picture Perfect/Rex Features; 75t John Kennedy O'Connor; 75b Sipa Press/Rex Features; 76 Michael Putland/Getty Images; 77t Peter Bischoff/Getty Images; 77b Chris Walter/Getty Images; 79 George Feston/Getty Images; 81t John Kennedy O'Connor; 81b Philip Jackson/Associated Newspapers/Rex Features; 82-83t Peter Bischoff/Getty Images; 83ml John Kennedy O'Connor; 83mr John Kennedy O'Connor; 83b Sipa Press/Rex Features; 84t Keystone/Getty Images; 84b John Kennedy O'Connor; 85 John Kennedy O'Connor; 86 Jorgen Angel/Getty Images; 87t David Fisher/Rex Features; 87b Rolf Klatt/Rex Features; 88 Poirier/Getty Images; 89t Frank Barratt/Getty Images; 89b Derek Cattani/Rex Features; 90-91 Dimitar Dilkoff/Getty Images; 92 Alinari/Rex Features; 93 Sten Rosenlund/Rex Features; 94 Rolf Klatt/Rex Features; 95t John Kennedy O'Connor; 95b Mustafa Ozer/Getty Images; 96l Sipa Press/Rex Features; 96r Peter Bischoff/Getty Images; 97t Johannes Simon/Getty Images; 97b Ragnar Singsaas/Getty Images; 98l Frank Leandros/Getty Images; 98-99b Vano Shlamov/AFP/Getty Images; 99t Johannes Simon/Getty Images; 100 Andrej Isakovic/Getty Images; 101 Peter Bischoff/Getty Images; 102 Keystone/Getty Images; 103t Geoffrey White/Daily Mail/Rex Features; 103b Peter Bischoff/Getty Images; 104t John Kennedy O'Connor; 104b Michael Putland/Getty Images; 105t Rolf Klatt/Rex Features; 105b Lehtikuva OY/Rex Features; 106-107 Derek Cattani/Rex Features; 107 Sean Gallup/Getty Images; 108 Keikki Saukkomaa/Rex Features; 109 Lehtikuva OY/Rex Features; 110-111t Sten Rosenlund/Rex Features; 111b Vyacheslav Oseledko/Getty Images; 112 Karin Tornblom/Rex Features; 113t Dimitar Dilkoff/Getty Images; 113b Central Press/Getty Images; 115t Sergei Supinsky/Getty Images; 115b Action Press/Rex Features; 116t Sari Gustafsson/Rex Features; 116b Keystone USA/VG/Rex Features; 117t Ari Ojala/Rex Features; 117b Action Press/Rex Features; 118 Hulton Archive/Getty Images; 119 Gianni Ferrari/Getty Images; 120-121 AFP/Getty Images.

Every effort has been made to acknowledge correctly and contact the source and/or copyright holder of each picture and Carlton Books Limited apologises for any unintentional errors or omissions, which will be, corrected in future editions of this book.

THIS IS A CARLTON BOOK

Published in Great Britain in 2015 by
Carlton Books Limited
20 Mortimer Street
London W1T 3JW

Text copyright © 2015 John Kennedy O'Connor
Design copyright © 2015 Carlton Books Limited
Eurovision, Eurovision logo and Eurovision Contest logos © 2015 EBU

"Eurovision", the Eurovision logo and Eurovision Song Contest logo are trade marks of the European Broadcasting Union and are used used under licence.

This book is sold subject to the condition that it shall not, by way of trade or otherwise, be lent, resold, hired out or otherwise circulated without the publisher's prior written consent in any form of cover or binding other than that in which it is published and without a similar condition including this condition, being imposed upon the subsequent purchaser. All rights reserved.

A CIP catalogue for this book is available from the British Library.

ISBN 978-1-78097-638-9

Printed in Dubai

10 9 8 7 6 5 4 3 2 1

THE EUROVISION
SONG CONTEST

THE OFFICIAL CELEBRATION

JOHN KENNEDY O'CONNOR

CARLTON
BOOKS

Contents

INTRODUCTION   **6**

CHAPTER ONE: "The Winner is…"   **8**
My Number One   10
We Are The Winners   14
Congratulations   18
Here Today, Gone Tomorrow   22
I'm Never Giving Up   24
What's Another Year?   28
Rock And Roll Kids   32
Lady, Lady   34
When?   36

CHAPTER TWO: Nul Points   **38**
Rock Bottom   40
Should've Known Better   44
Don't Play That Song Again   48
All Out Of Luck   52
Cry Baby   54
That Sounds Good To Me   56
Rise Like A Phoenix   58
Why Do I Always Get It Wrong?   60
It's Just A Game   62

CHAPTER THREE: Hosting & Voting   **64**
That's What Friends Are For   66
If I Could Choose   68
Are You Sure?   70
The Party's Over Now   72
Somewhere In Europe   74
On Again… Off Again   76
Come Back To Stay   78
Parlez-Vous Français?   80

Happy Man   82
Making Your Mind Up   86
Mister Music Man   88

CHAPTER FOUR: Weird & Wonderful   90
Wild Dances   92
You Got Style   96
I Love The Little Things   98
Sing Little Birdie   100
Let Me Be The One   102
Ding Ding-A-Dong   104
Boom Boom Boomerang   106
All Kinds Of Everything   108
La La La…   110
A Little Peace   112
Flying The Flag   114
Hard Rock Hallelujah   116
Absent Friends   118

CHAPTER FIVE: Records   120
Most Successful Songs by Nation   122
Overall Records   127

Artists around the scoreboard for the 1963 Eurovision contest.

Introduction

This celebration captures the flavour of Eurovision, charting its journey from the first competition in 1956 with just seven entrants and a live audience of only 200, broadcast from a casino in Switzerland, to the international extravaganza watched by billions of viewers that it is today.

Believe it or not, the Eurovision Song Contest was designed to "stimulate the output of original high quality songs in the field of popular music by encouraging competition between authors and composers through the international comparison of their works." Despite giving the world 'Boom Bang-A-Bang' and 'Diggi-Loo, Diggi-Ley', that mission statement really is the objective of one of the most adored, maligned, popular and longest-running television shows ever broadcast. Costing millions of Euros to produce, it is watched today by hundreds of millions of viewers across the globe, who love it or loathe it in equal measure.

In this book, you'll discover all the stories, facts and fun that have kept viewers enthralled for sixty years. In that time, 26 nations have won the contest from a field of 51 countries

John Kennedy O'Connor announces the scores for San Marino at Eurovision 2013.

S/EPIC · THE MUSIC PEOPLE AT EUROVISION:1974
Epic

Brighton 1974: ABBA, Gigliola Cinquetti, Piera Martell – and The Wombles.

to have entered, some from well beyond Europe's borders, some no longer in existence, and some that did not exist at all when the first contest was staged in 1956, in the Swiss city of Lugano. You'll find out once and for all if Norway truly is Eurovision's most hopeless nation despite their three wins; if Serbia-Montenegro actually is statistically the best; and learn if genteel socialite Katie Boyle really did "go commando" to host the contest in 1974.

Furthermore, have you ever wondered just how hard it is to say "douze points" live to 195 million viewers from a tiny studio in San Marino or to commentate to millions of viewers watching live all over the world? I am grateful to the contest I've loved for over 40 years for letting me figure those last two out for myself. For the rest, the answers are all here in the *Eurovision Song Contest: The Official Celebration*.

John Kennedy O'Connor, 2015

Tom Neuwirth's bearded alter ego Conchita Wurst triumphs in 2014, helping Austria 'Rise Like A Phoenix' to their second victory a record 48 years after their last.

— CHAPTER ONE —

"The Winner is…"

From million sellers to one-hit wonders,
skirt-ripping popstars to scary monster rockers,
the world's greatest singing competition
has seen it all… and so much more.

My Number One

ENTRIES AND ENTRANTS THAT BECAME HITS

The first two Eurovision Song Contests provided little in the way of commercial success for any of the competing songs, let alone the actual winners. All this changed in 1958 when a song overlooked by the juries went on to become one of the biggest hits of the year and, indeed, of all time.

Winning Italy's San Remo Festival earned Domenico Modugno a global hit with 'Volare', and took him to the top of the US singles chart.

THE MOST IMPORTANT SONG

'Volare' ('To Fly') won the San Remo Music Festival as 'Nel Blu Di Pinto Di Blu' ('In The Sky Painted Blue') and, already No. 1 in the Italian chart, went forward to Hilversum as Italy's entry performed by its writer, **Domenico Modugno**. The song placed 3rd but was soon No. 1 in the USA for five weeks and was awarded Grammy Awards for "Record of the Year" and "Song of the Year". The track has reportedly sold 22 million copies to date, providing hits for **Bobby Rydell**, **Dean Martin**, **Dalida**, **Andrea Bocelli** and **The Gipsy Kings**. 'Volare' can possibly be regarded as the most important Eurovision song ever. It demonstrated what the contest was capable of producing and encouraged 60 years of hopeful writers.

CHART TOPPER

Italy really had the hang of finding songs that the public loved but the juries were blasé about, at best. Their 1960 entry was another global hit, but another song the Eurovision judges overlooked. Composer **Renato Rascel** finished 8th in the London contest with 'Romantica' ('Romance') and took his version to the top of the Italian and French charts. American star **Jane Morgan** recorded an English version of the song and was soon crashing into the hit parades all over Europe and beyond.

Renato Rascel placed 8th in London 1960 with 'Romantica', yet remained one of Italy's leading entertainers.

THIS IS MY SONG

The first true smash-hit, winning single didn't come until Eurovision's ninth contest in 1964, when at last the juries agreed with the public that Italy had the best song. 'Non Ho L'Età' ('I Am Too Young') earned 16-year-old **Gigliola Cinquetti** a runaway victory in Copenhagen and a No. 1 hit in Belgium, France, Italy and the Netherlands and No. 3 hits in Germany and Norway. Even in the UK, where hits for non-English songs were exceptionally rare, the single reached No. 17. Ironically, the British record buyers preferred Gigliola's 1974 runner up 'Si' ('Yes'), which was a No. 8 hit in the UK as 'Go'. 1964's winner was recorded by **Dame Vera Lynn** as 'This Is My Prayer' but didn't reach the charts.

SINGING DOLL

Serge Gainsbourg brought his Svengali touch to 1965's Eurovision in Naples, penning Luxembourg's winner 'Poupée De Cire, Poupée De Son' ('Wax Doll, Singing Doll') for **France Gall**. The song was soon a smash hit all over Europe and beyond, hitting No. 1 in Norway and French-speaking Canada and the Top 5 in France, Luxembourg, Germany, Belgium, Finland, Japan and Singapore. **Twinkle** tried to take the English version into the UK charts, but failed. Other hit versions – in Arabic, Czech, Danish, Dutch, Estonian, Hebrew, Japanese, Korean, Russian and Vietnamese, to name but a few – soon followed. France Gall became a major star in Asia but turned out to be the first Eurovision winner to disassociate herself from the contest and refuses to discuss it in any medium today.

NO STRINGS

'Puppet On A String' was the first British Eurovision winner and the first song from the contest to top the UK singles chart, which it did for three weeks. Soon after crushing all opposition in Vienna, barefoot **Sandie Shaw** also reached No. 1 in Austria, Germany, Ireland and Norway, earning her the biggest-selling single of the year in each of those territories. Sandie's version went global, but many other imitations followed, including covers by **Siw Malmkvist**, **Ken Boothe**, **Mantovani** and **Anneke Grönloh**. **Lele** even hit with it in Lithuanian.

CONGRATULATIONS

The song was written as 'I Think I Love You', but lyricist **Bill Martin** was told by composer **Phil Coulter** that the words were "a load of rubbish", so he quickly came up with 'Congratulations' instead. **Cliff Richard** narrowly failed to top the Eurovision voting, but that didn't stop the song clocking up sales in excess of 1,000,000 copies and becoming a global hit. Cliff recorded Spanish, German and French lyrics for the track as well as releasing the English version all over Europe and in the USA, where it cracked the *Billboard* Hot 100. 'Congratulations' has become a standard, sung whenever celebrations are called for.

TWO MILLION COPY HIT

Ireland's first contest winner, 'All Kinds Of Everything' in 1970, sparked sales of over 2 million units for **Dana**, including an amazing 100,000 in Ireland alone, where it topped the charts for 9 weeks, both records at the time. Scoring two weeks at No. 1 in the UK, Dana also hit big in the Netherlands (where the contest was staged, in Amsterdam), Austria, Germany, Israel, Malaysia, Singapore, New Zealand, South Africa and Yugoslavia, where the track hit the Top 10 in each territory.

London-born Rosemary Brown became Ireland's first Eurovision winner Dana in 1970, setting a record for scoring 9 out of 10 points from the Belgian jury.

PURE GOLD

ABBA's 'Waterloo' may not officially be the biggest-selling winning single in the contest's history, but there can be no argument that it has been purchased more than any other song ever to enter the competition, let alone win. The single alone reached sales of 6,000,000, officially reaching No. 1 in competing countries Belgium, Finland, Ireland, the UK, the Netherlands, Norway and Switzerland and in non-competing Denmark and South Africa. Top 10 success also came in Sweden, Spain, Rhodesia, New Zealand, France, Canada, Austria and Australia. It is included on two of the most successful greatest hits albums of all time (*ABBA Greatest Hits* – 1976 and *ABBA Gold* – 1992) as well as countless other compilations; combined sales of those two albums alone are estimated at 40 million units. No wonder 'Waterloo' was named Eurovision's greatest ever song at the 50th anniversary celebration 'Congratulations' in 2005.

OH BROTHER!

'Save Your Kisses For Me' told the twee tale of a guy leaving his sweetheart behind, only for the denouement of the song to reveal it was a father saying goodbye to his 3-year-old daughter. The sentiment took **Brotherhood of Man** to No. 1 for six weeks in the UK, earning them the biggest hit of 1976 with sales way in excess of 1,000,000. They also scored the highest relative score in the contest's history under the "douze points" system introduced in 1975. Although many higher scores have been recorded since, the UK's 1976 winner got a record 164 points out of the possible total 204 available, a staggering 80.39%. Another 5,000,000 sales followed across the globe.

GERMANY GOES NUMBER ONE

'Ein Bißchen Frieden' ('A Little Peace') was the runaway winner in 1982 for **Nicole**, scoring Germany's long awaited first Eurovision victory. Nicole already had her eye on the international charts when she reprised her victory singing in German, English, French and Dutch at the end of the show and was very soon No. 1 not only in Germany but in the UK, the Netherlands, Ireland, Austria, Norway, Sweden and Switzerland. Cover versions flooded the market, to compete with Nicole's own versions recorded in German, English, Italian, Spanish, Japanese, Dutch and Danish.

FIZZY HIT

The debut single from **Bucks Fizz** only narrowly won Eurovision in 1981, the only winner under the "douze points" system to score just two top marks. It was much clearer that the public agreed 'Making Your Mind Up' was the winner when it ascended the hit parade across the continent. No. 1 hits came in the UK, the Netherlands, Ireland, Austria, Belgium, Spain, Israel and Denmark with Top 10 successes in Sweden, Norway, Switzerland and Germany. Further afield, the track reached the Top 10 in New Zealand, Australia and South Africa. BBC Radio 2 listeners voted the track as the best-ever British Eurovision entry in 2013.

SATELLITE OF LOVE

Lena's 'Satellite' won in 2010, went to No. 1 in six countries and was certified gold and platinum in at least four. **Loreen**'s 'Euphoria' was the biggest success from the contest in decades, reaching No. 1 in Austria, Belgium, Denmark, Estonia, Finland, Germany, Greece, Iceland, Ireland, Norway, Poland, Russia, Sweden, Slovakia, Switzerland and going Top 10 in Australia, Bulgaria, Croatia, The Czech Republic, Israel, the Netherlands, Hungary, Moldova, Portugal, Romania, Spain, Turkey, Ukraine and the UK.

Brotherhood of Man still hold the record for the highest relative score under the "douze points" voting system, earning 80.39% of the available points.

We Are The Winners

SURPRISE WINNERS

Eurovision wouldn't be Eurovision without a shock result: not every chart-topper from the contest was picked by the judges.

OH LA LA LA!

Surprise winners abound at Eurovision, but perhaps none more than **Massiel** from Spain. Originally, **Joan Manuel Serrat** was selected to represent Spain at the 1968 contest with 'La, La, La…'. However, his intention to perform the song in Catalan was blocked by bosses at Spain's TVE and a replacement artist quickly sought. A call went out to Mexico, where Massiel was touring and she leapt at the chance, promising that if they gave her the opportunity to sing for Spain, she would win the contest. To almost everyone's amazement (and much disgust) she was right.

JUST A LITTLE BIT

Although Ireland hadn't technically won the 1995 contest, ending the nation's run of three consecutive victories, **Secret Garden**'s **Fionnuala Sherry** had ensured the Irish made it four in a row anyway. Nobody saw another victory for Ireland coming in 1996, least of all Britain's **Gina G**. 'Ooh Aah… Just A Little Bit' had been a major UK hit in the weeks running up to the contest in Oslo and indeed had moved to No. 1 the day of the competition. The song was the red hot favourite to win, but alas, singing second proved fatal and Gina slumped to 8th place, while the rank outsider **Eimear Quinn** cruised to a win with 'The Voice'.

Australian Gina G topped the charts and earned a Grammy nomination, but Eurovision glory eluded her.

REPEAT TO FADE

Norway's second victory was another surprise. **Secret Garden** triumphed with 'Nocturne' in 1995, although the exact configuration of the group's membership was just one confusion. Norwegian **Rolf Løvland** and Ireland's **Fionnuala Sherry** were the main focus of the act but for the performance, two musicians, **Asa Jinder** on the keyfiddle and **Hans Fredrik Jacobsen** on whistle, were drafted in, as well as the singer, **Gunnhild Tvinnereim**, who was there to perform the lyric – what there was of it. 'Nocturne' had only 24 words in seven lines of lyrics.

CHART TOPPER

Following **ABBA**'s victory in 1974, almost every subsequent Swedish entry was overshadowed by their most successful export. Teenager **Carola** seemed to shake ABBA's ghost off her back in 1983 to place 3rd with 'Främling' ('Stranger'), but nobody was expecting anything like as good a finish the following year when the Mormon, American-based **Herreys** brothers, **Per, Richard & Louis**, donned their golden boots and opened the show in Luxembourg. 'Diggi-Loo, Diggi-Ley' may have set the contest back lyrically by as much as a decade, but the brothers' choreography set new standards of polish and complexity.

ONE NIGHT'S ANGER

Estonia's **Dave Benton & Tanel Padar** joined forces to sing 'Everybody' in 2001 for a nation that was steadily improving in the contest after a pretty insignificant start. Nobody predicted their victory, which seemed to catch the two artists as much by surprise as anyone else. Within days of their win, they were not on speaking terms, let alone willing to sing their winning song together. Although they did appear briefly to reprise 'Everybody' at the start of the 2002 contest in Tallinn, that was their only appearance together after returning from Copenhagen a year earlier. Needless to say, a follow up is probably out of the question.

HI-ENERGY

Israeli actress and singer **Ofra Haza** was a huge star in the Middle Eeast long before coming to München in 1983 to perform 'Hi' ('Alive'), a defiant song telling the world that Israel was thriving despite all its historic challenges with Germany. Although Ofra finished 2nd, her career continued to build around the world and she became by far the most globally recognized star of the class of 1983. Whatever happened to the singer that beat her to Eurovision glory, **Corinne Hermès** winning for Luxembourg, isn't at all clear.

UNLUCKY THIRTEEN

Germany's **Lale Andersen** was the original 'Lili Marleen' of the Second World War, the song becoming enormously popular with serving German soldiers and even scoring a huge hit with the opposing sides. Despite its huge popularity, **Joseph Goebbels** banned the song. When Lale arrived at Eurovision 1961, she met up with the Allied Forces' sweetheart **Dame Vera Lynn** for the first time, before performing 'Einmal Sehen Wir Uns Wieder' ('Once We'll Meet Again') as the oldest singer (at 56 years of age) to take part in the contest until 2008.

TOP OF THE POPS

Britain has never produced another star of **Sir Cliff Richard**'s success and longevity. For over 50 years, he's been a fixture of the British entertainment and pop scene. Yet at Eurovision, Cliff's fame didn't help him secure a win, no matter how many times he tried. In 1968, he took up the offer from the BBC to sing for Britain only when his friend **Cilla Black** had turned it down. 'Congratulations' gave him a global, chart-topping hit, but he was pipped by one point at the contest. He tried again in 1973 and again tripped up (quite literally when the microphone cable became entwined in his legs during some bizarre choreography) dropping to 3rd with 'Power To All Our Friends' but still outselling the winning song by two to one.

Cilla Black congratulates her pal Cliff Richard as Bill Martin and Phil Coulter win a second UK heat in a row with 'Congratulations'.

HEARTBREAK HOTEL

Toše Proeski was enjoying superstardom across the Balkans when his Eurovision opportunity for FYR Macedonia came in 2004. His song 'Life' didn't score well beyond his regional support, but his career ascendancy continued, with UNICEF appointing him a goodwill ambassador. He was dubbed the "Elvis Presley of the Balkans", but his career was tragically ended in a freak car accident in 2007. Such was his star status that he was given a state funeral, attended by many global leaders.

Todor "Toše" Proeski tried several times to represent FYR Macedonia, finally reaching Eurovision in 2004 with 'Life', placing 14th.

RUSSIAN STARLET

Alla Pugacheva's appearance at Eurovision in 1997 delighted her millions of Russian and former Soviet fans, even if her song 'Prima Donna' left the voters cold. An actress, singer and song writer, Pugacheva enjoyed superstar status from her earliest recordings to the present day and is often cited as the biggest-selling Russian artist in history, also ranking amongst the Top 20 biggest-selling global stars.

GREEK GODDESS

Greek stars **Nana Mouskouri** and **Vicky Leandros** had both represented Luxembourg at Eurovision and so, not surprisingly, Greece's leading female star **Marinella** was asked to perform the country's debut Eurovision entry in 1974. 'Krassi Thalassa Ke T'Agori Mou' ('Wine, Sea, My Boyfriend And Me') did little to impress, but its failure did nothing to impair Marinella's superstardom. She remains an icon of Greek cinema and music and was chosen to close the 2004 Olympics in Athens.

Greece's Nana Mouskouri sang in French for Luxembourg in 1963, placing 8th. Curiously, it was this Eurovision failure that led to worldwide success.

Congratulations

EUROVISION'S MOST SUCCESSFUL ACTS

Eurovision has done much to launch, cement and indeed revive careers, but probably none more so than a Swedish quartet originally known as **Björn & Benny and Anna & Frida**.

THANK YOU FOR THE MUSIC

ABBA was made up of two couples (**Agnetha & Björn** and **Benny & Anni-Frid**) who failed to qualify for Eurovision 1973 with a song called 'Ring Ring'. Having dialled the wrong Eurovision number, the contest and indeed the world of pop music may never have been the same again, had they not returned to meet their 'Waterloo' and triumph in the 1974 contest. Within 18 months they were in danger of eclipsing **The Beatles** as the most successful pop group ever.

Bringing modern glam rock to the Brighton stage, Sweden's newly renamed ABBA triumphed with 'Waterloo' by just 6 points.

In the closest contest since 1968, Canada's Céline Dion wins for Switzerland in 1988.

CELINE DION

SUIÇA
Eurovisão
1 9 8 8
DUBLIN

"ne partez pas sans moi"

BECAUSE WE LOVED HER

A French Canadian songstress, who had found early success as a teenager, was chosen to represent Switzerland at the 1988 contest in Dublin. **Céline Dion** (for it was she) arrived in the Irish capital as the clear favourite but found herself lagging behind Britain's **Scott Fitzgerald**, a Scottish one-hit wonder from a decade earlier, in the voting. Scott's 'Go' seemed to be cruising to victory when the Portuguese jury closed the gap to just 5 points, leaving Yugoslavia to decide the contest. Yugoslavia's 6 points to Céline gave her a 1-point win and soon she was learning English in readiness for conquering the music world.

BROTHERS IN ARMS

Despite a couple of fairly substantial hits early in the decade, **Brotherhood of Man** had undergone so many personnel changes by 1976, and so many changes in fortune, that they were largely forgotten in the UK music scene. All that changed when **Martin Lee, Lee Sheridan** and the unrelated **Nicky and Sandra Stevens** conquered Europe with their self-penned 'Save Your Kisses For Me'. The first Eurovision entry ever to top the UK charts before reaching the contest finals, they arrived in Den Haag the hot favourites and despite a rather meagre score from the Irish jury, clinched victory with the biggest relative score ever achieved under the "douze points" voting system, a record they maintain right up to the 60th anniversary. Pioneers of choreographic excellence (or criminality, you decide), the foursome remained top of the pops for several years after scoring the biggest-selling winning single in the contest's entire history and remain together as a working band to this day.

In 1976, the UK's Brotherhood of Man ran away with the contest, 'Save Your Kisses For Me' being the second consecutive winner to be performed first.

RIPPING IT UP!

Five years after Britain's **Brotherhood of Man** had won Eurovision, music producer **Andy Hill** formed **Bucks Fizz** to sing 'Making Your Mind Up' at the contest in Dublin. **Cheryl Baker**, the former member of disastrously unsuccessful band **Co-Co**, teamed up with **Mike Nolan, Bobby G** and **Jay Aston**, and the group worked hard on the choreography of their jive routine with the daring skirt-rip move midway through – perhaps at the detriment of their vocals, which veered dangerously off-key on the Eurovision stage. The poor singing proved irrelevant, as they eked out a 4-point victory over the better-tipped German entry 'Johnny Blue' and set forth on a hugely successful career that spanned several decades.

GRAND NANA

Greece didn't enter Eurovision until 1974, by which time, two of its most famous artists had already tried their hand on behalf of Luxembourg. **Nana Mouskouri** didn't trouble the juries too much in 1963, limping home half way down the scoreboard with 'À Force De Prier' ('The Power Of Prayer'). Her compatriot **Vicky Leandros** finished 4th in 1967, but missed out on the global hit that ensued for **Paul Mauriat** with her entry 'L'Amour Est Bleu' ('Love Is Blue'). Her next Eurovision effort was rejected by Germany but snapped up by Luxembourg, leading to her victory in Edinburgh, 1972 with 'Après Toi' ('After You') and this time, the global hit was hers.

Sandie Shaw scored Eurovision's biggest seller of the 1960s but despised her winner 'Puppet On A String' and for many years, refused to sing it at all.

SHAW THING

Before Britain started selecting unknown groups or singers for Eurovision duty, the BBC generally sent household names to represent the nation abroad. **Sandie Shaw** and **Lulu** were two such stars who certainly had no need of the contest, but who accepted the invitation nonetheless and both took home gold. Sandie's popularity stumbled as a result of the enormous success of her winner 'Puppet On A String', which outsold and overshadowed her entire previous career, leading to her spending years denigrating the contest and its entire works. **Lulu** pretty much carried on as before, despite not being too enamoured of her winner 'Boom Bang-A-Bang'.

NICOLE AND LENA

Germany had to wait until 1982 to finally notch up a Eurovision win, making a domestic star of **Nicole**, who scored a truly international hit with her winner 'Ein Bißchen Frieden' ('A Little Peace'). Twenty-eight years later, **Lena Meyer-Landrut** was plucked from obscurity through a TV talent show in an attempt to reverse the fortunes of the Big Five's least successful nation. Lena easily won *Unser Star Für Oslo (Our Star For Oslo)*, with the song 'Satellite' and such was its popularity that it immediately topped the German charts, becoming the country's fastest-selling digital release ever, attaining 100,000 sales in its first week.

After a wait of 28 years, Germany scored a second victory in 2010 thanks to Lena Meyer-Landrut's 'Satellite'.

POWER TO THE PEOPLE

Two Eurovision winners enjoyed enormous chart success before turning their backs on music for the world of politics. **Dana** was the first of Ireland's seven victors in 1970 and was a regular hit maker for the next decade. Ukraine's **Ruslana**, already a domestic superstar, took Europe by storm in 2004 with 'Wild Dances' but was soon embroiled in the Orange Revolution that swept **Viktor Yuschenko** to power later in the year. Her popularity soared and she soon found herself elected to the newly democratic Ukrainian Parliament.

Александр Рыбак
Fairytale

BEST OF WURST?

Only time will tell if recent Eurovision winners **Alexander Rybak, Loreen, Emmelie De Forest** or **Conchita Wurst** can consolidate their initial successes. For Rybak, the Belarusian-born singer who set new records whilst storming to victory for Norway in 2009, things don't look promising. One of only three winners to accompany themselves on violin, the first as lead singer – a novelty that no act since has tried to emulate yet – he continues to grab Scandinavian headlines, more for his infamous temper tantrums than his musical successes.

Here Today, Gone Tomorrow

ONE-HIT WONDERS

A top finish in the Eurovision Song Contest can mean instant stardom, but not all contestants have the luck or staying power to remain in the spotlight of fame…

Global chart-topper Mary Hopkin boards the flight for Amsterdam, where finishing 2nd ends her success.

HOP, SKIP AND JUMP

Mary Hopkin was enjoying considerable success after winning a British TV talent show in 1968. Topping the charts across Europe with 'Those Were The Days', she also found success with her follow-ups in 1969, including breaking the US market, and her future seemed golden. Finishing 2nd at Eurovision 1970 with 'Knock, Knock (Who's There?)' put paid to that. Despite a big hit with the single of her entry and repeated attempts to reinvent herself, Mary was rarely heard of again. She took the knocks well, but later freely admitted how much she despised the song and the contest.

DANCE WITH THE DEVIL

Liverpool lass **Sonia** shot to the top of the UK charts with her debut single and into the US Dance Chart Top 10, while her first album went gold. She leapt at the chance to represent the UK when the BBC invited her to sing in Millstreet, 1993 and despite predictions of gloom from **Terry Wogan**, she dazzled the audience, with 'Better The Devil You Know'. It seemed early on in the voting that Sonia's genuinely impressive performance of the song had won the judges' hearts and she looked to be cruising to victory. Alas, in part thanks to the British judges themselves, Ireland's home entry closed the gap and edged ahead in the final rounds of voting, stealing victory on the last scores from Malta. Viewers watched as Sonia was visibly crushed and sadly for the hit maker, 'Better The Devil You Know' was also the last time she troubled the charts.

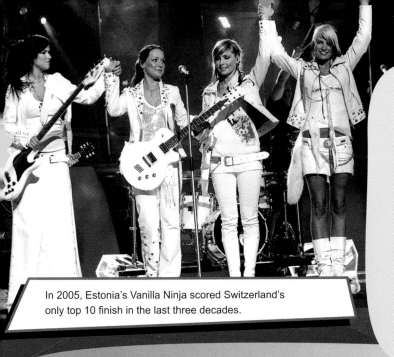

In 2005, Estonia's Vanilla Ninja scored Switzerland's only top 10 finish in the last three decades.

COOL NINJAS

Estonian girl band **Vanilla Ninja** tried to represent their homeland more than once, but despite their success domestically, they never did get to sing for their country. Instead, having found much success in continental Europe, they were picked to sing for Switzerland in 2005. Well, if it was good enough for a French Canadian… The girls' song about a tiger, 'Cool Vibes', finished 8th, a great result for the Swiss, but they were soon after dropped by their label and personnel changes left the group badly damaged.

BACCARA

Spanish duo **Maria & Mayte** came to Paris 1978 as **Baccara** and as the favourites to triumph, largely due to their hot streak of pan-European chart toppers. Born in Spain, the pair was based in Germany, working with French impresario **Rolf Soja** and Belgian **Frank Dorstal**, and signed to American record label RCA. Naturally, they were chosen to represent Luxembourg to sing in French. The song 'Parlez Vous Français?' ('Do You Speak French?') was perhaps too close to their hits 'Yes Sir! I Can Boogie' and 'Sorry, I'm A Lady' for the judges' comfort and they slumped to 7th place. Maria & Mayte split, but each formed a new **Baccara** with a new partner. Yes, be afraid; there really are two **Baccaras** out there.

Silver Convention were the world's biggest-selling female group, but 'Telegram' failed to deliver.

LOSING SILVER

German female trio **Silver Convention** were enjoying global success from 1975 onwards when their track 'Fly Robin, Fly' topped the American singles chart for three weeks, scoring the first ever US No. 1 for a German act. They picked up a Grammy award, topped the Canadian charts and racked up the hits at home and abroad with 'Save Me', 'Get Up And Boogie' and 'Everybody's Talking 'Bout Love'. 'Telegram' went to London as Germany's 1977 song for Eurovision, and after placing 8th that was pretty much the last time the group ever troubled the record-buying public. They struggled through 1978 and split up in 1979.

I'm Never Giving Up

THE WINNERS WHO CAME BACK FOR MORE

It is clear that some contestants can't get enough of Eurovision,
so much so that some have entered once, twice, three times!

SWISS LYS

Lys Assia won the first ever Eurovision Song Contest, but
victory wasn't enough for Swiss Lys. Flushed with her success,
she returned in 1957 to defend her title, but couldn't manage
better than one place above last. Not deterred, Ms. Assia
almost got her double the following year in Hilversum, when
she switched from singing in French to Italian, but ended 2nd
with her song about 'Giorgio'. Voting last, the Italians pushed
her into second place in favour of the French song. Lys should
have stuck to her first language.

"I was the only Swiss singer possible to
defend the country," said Lys Assia modestly.

WE LOVE YOU

Suave boulevardier Frenchman
Jean-Claude Pascal was
invited to cross the border to
sing for Luxembourg in 1961
and triumphed with 'Nous Les
Amoureaux' ('We Who Love
Each Other'). A successful actor,
Jean-Claude sang in a very
similar vein to other famous
French actors **Louis Jourdan**
and **Maurice Chevalier**. Twenty
years later, Jean-Claude returned
for Luxembourg in 1981, but the
contest had moved on in style and
he placed 11th, way behind the
skirt-ripping **Bucks Fizz.**

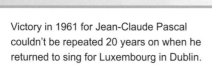

Victory in 1961 for Jean-Claude Pascal
couldn't be repeated 20 years on when he
returned to sing for Luxembourg in Dublin.

THREE IN A ROW

Isabelle Aubret scored France's third Eurovision winner in five years in 1962, making it the first nation to score a trio of victories. 'Un Premier Amour' ('A First Love') was a runaway winner, but it is Isabelle's next effort, 'La Source' ('The Source'), that is generally critically the better regarded of her two entries, despite the latter finishing only 3rd in 1968. Isabelle made further attempts to sing for France, but she never got beyond the domestic heats.

JUST SAY YES

Gigliola Cinquetti told the world she was too young to love with her 1964 winner and by the time she came back to Eurovision exactly ten years later, she certainly had matured. Sung last in Brighton, 'Si' ('Yes') gave **ABBA**'s 'Waterloo' a very close run, despite viewers in Italy not being allowed to watch the contest live because it was thought the lyric might influence a referendum on divorce. Gigliola returned to Eurovision a third time, as co-host of the 1991 contest in Rome.

Isabelle Aubret triumphed in 1962, France becoming the first nation to score three victories. In 1968, she had to settle for 3rd place.

NUMBER ONE FOR TWO

Vicky Leandros moved up from 4th in 1967 to victory in 1972 for Luxembourg and was present when **Anne-Marie David** made it two in a row for the Grand Duchy the following year on home ground with 'Tu Te Reconnaîtras' ('You'll Recognize Yourself'). Anne-Marie returned to the contest in 1979, this time representing her native France, the first winning singer to represent two countries. She scored heavily in the early voting and a double win seemed possible, but eventually she had to settle for 3rd place with 'Je Suis L'Enfant Du Soleil' ('I Am A Child Of The Sun').

HERE'S JOHNNY

Although **Lys Assia** and **Gigliola Cinquetti** had come very, very close, it was Australian/Irishman **Johnny Logan** who became the first (and officially only) singer to win Eurovision twice. Triumphing in 1980 with **Shay Healy**'s 'What's Another Year?' Johnny returned in 1987 with his own composition 'Hold Me Now' and romped home to victory once more. In the interim years, he'd composed **Linda Martin**'s 'Terminal Three', which placed 2nd in 1984, and wrote another song for her in 1992, 'Why Me?'. This time, Linda got her win and Johnny got his third victory.

Ireland's "Mr. Eurovision" Johnny Logan won twice as a singer and twice as a composer, for a total of three wins.

BAKER'S DOZEN

Cheryl Baker had made it her life's ambition to win Eurovision, but when her group **Co-Co** placed 11th in the 1978 contest with 'The Bad Old Days', it was the UK's worst result to date and she swore she'd never do it again. Three years later, she was in the line-up for newly formed **Bucks Fizz** and went to Dublin to fulfill her dream. It was the best improvement for any winning singer in the contest's history until **Hanne Krogh** moved up from 17th to win with **Bobbysocks**. Both members of Bobbysocks, **Hanne** and **Elisabeth Andreassen**, took part in Eurovision in other guises (and in Elisabeth's case for another country) before and after winning the contest for Norway. Elisabeth came closest to winning again in 1996, when she became the fourth singer to both win the contest and finish 2nd.

NO HERO

Young **Carola** placed 3rd for Sweden in 1983 before winning out in 1991. **Charlotte Nilsson Perreli** tried it the other way round, winning in 1999 with 'Take Me To Your Heaven' in Jerusalem, but when she came back in 2008 in Belgrade, she qualified only thanks to the jury vote and slipped to 18th in the final with 'Hero', the worst showing yet for a former winner. She hasn't yet returned, whereas Carola did try again, only to place 5th in 2006.

Sweden's Carola snatched victory from France in 1991 thanks to a tie-breaker. In 2005, she managed only defeat.

IT'S ALL FOR YOU

Ireland's **Niamh Kavanagh** was clearly keen to rob her countryman **Johnny Logan** of his status as the only two-time winner, returning to the contest in 2010, some seventeen years after she'd won in Millstreet with 'In Your Eyes'. Her second effort, 'It's For You' was highly thought of in the run-up to the Oslo contest, yet Niamh could only better **Charlotte Nilsson**'s dubious achievement by slumping to 23rd place, two from the bottom. Other than **Corry Brokken**'s last of 10 entrants, this was the worst-ever result for a former contest winner.

WIND UP!

Although they never won the contest at all, it's perhaps worth noting that German group **Wind** hold the distinction of being the only Eurovision act ever to finish 2nd twice. Not content with this record, they made a third attempt to go one better in 1992, only to place 16th with 'Träume Sind Für Alle Da'. Perhaps 'Dreams Are Made For Everyone' is not true after all. Spare a thought and have a heart for Norwegian **Anne Karine Strøm**, the only singer in Eurovision history to finish last twice.

BEST RECORDS OF PERFORMERS

ALL PERFORMERS WHO HAVE COMPETED ON MORE THAN ONE OCCASION AND HAVE PLACED IN THE TOP THREE AT LEAST ONCE.

JOHNNY LOGAN	1st 1980, 1st 1987
ELISABETH ANDREASSEN~	1st 1985, 2nd 1996, 6th 1994, 8th 1982
LYS ASSIA	1st 1956, 2nd 1958, 8th 1957, UNPLACED 1956
GIGLIOLA CINQUETTI	1st 1964, 2nd 1974
LINDA MARTIN	1st 1992, 2nd 1984
DIMA BILAN	1st 2008, 2nd 2006
CAROLA	1st 1991, 3rd 1983, 5th 2006
ISABELLE AUBRET	1st 1962, 3rd 1968
ANNE-MARIE DAVID∞	1st 1973, 3rd 1979
HELENA PAPARIZOU++	1st 2005, 3rd 2001
UDO JÜRGENS	1st 1966, 4th 1965, 6th 1964
VICKY LEANDROS	1st 1972, 4th 1967
IZHAR COHEN^	1st 1978, 5th 1985
CORRY BROKKEN	1st 1957, =9th 1957, UNPLACED 1956
LENA MEYER-LANDRUT	1st 2010, 10th 2011
JEAN CLAUDE PASCAL	1st 1961, 11th 1981
CHERYL BAKER*	1st 1981, 11th 1978
HANNE KROGH+	1st 1985, 17th 1971, 17th 1991
CHARLOTTE NILSSON PERRELLI	1st 1999, 18th 2008
NIAMH KAVANAGH	1st 1993, 23rd 2010
WIND	2nd 1985, 2nd 1987, 15th 1992
KATJA EBSTEIN	2nd 1980, 3rd 1970, 3rd 1971
FRANCOIS DEGUELT	2nd 1962, 3rd 1960
CLIFF RICHARD	2nd 1968, 3rd 1973
CHIARA	2nd 2005, 3rd 1998, 22nd 2009
ŽELJKO JOKSIMOVIĆ ◊	2nd 2004, 3rd 2012
JEAN VALLÉE	2nd 1978, =8th 1970
ROMUALD Φ	3rd 1964, =4th 1974, 11th 1969
HOT EYES	3rd 1988, 4th 1984, 11th 1985
DOMENICO MODUGNO	3rd 1958, 6th 1959, =17th 1966
SALLY-ANN TRIPLETT †	3rd 1980, 7th 1982
SAKIS ROUVAS	3rd 2004, 7th 2009
KIKKI DANIELSSON‡	3rd 1985, 8th 1982
THE SWARBRIGGS>	3rd 1977, 9th 1975
ŞEBNEM PAKER<	3rd 1997, 12th 1996
CAMILLO FELGEN	3rd 1962, 13th 1960
MARY ROOS	3rd 1972, =13th 1984

~AS PART OF SWEDEN'S CHIPS 1982, NORWAY'S BOBBYSOCKS 1985, WITH JAN WERNER 1994 AND AS A SOLOIST 1996
∞LUXEMBOURG 1973 AND FRANCE 1979
^AS LEAD SINGER OF ALPHA-BETA 1978 AND AS A SOLOIST 1985
*AS PART OF CO-CO 1978 AND BUCKS FIZZ 1981
+AS A SOLOIST 1971, WITH BOBBYSOCKS 1985 AND WITH JUST 4 FUN 1991
ΦMONACO 1964 AND 1974, LUXEMBOURG 1969
◊ SERBIA & MONTENEGRO 2004 AND SERBIA 2012
†WITH PRIMA DONNA IN 1980 AND AS PART OF BARDO IN 1982
‡AS A SOLOIST IN 1985 AND AS PART OF CHIPS IN 1982
>AS THE SWARBRIGGS IN 1975 AND AS THE SWARBRIGGS PLUS TWO IN 1977
< AS A SOLOIST IN 1996 AND WITH THE GROUP ETNIC IN 1997
++AS A SOLOIST IN 2005 AND WITH ANTIQUE IN 2001

What's Another Year?

THE ARTISTS APPEARING TWICE IN A ROW

Many singers have won Eurovision at their second, even third attempts, but generally there's been a decent interval between attempts. Others just can't seem to kick the habit and have come back for more in consecutive contests.

THIRD TIME LUCKY

Austria has something of a habit of sending artists to back-to-back contests. **Udo Jürgens** made it three in a row and triumphed third time lucky, but **Marty Bremm** wasn't quite so fortunate. He appeared with **Blue Danube** in 1980, and the group did pretty well to place 8th, but when he ditched his fellow singers and returned solo in 1981 with a motley crew of backing singers, including a woman in a leotard and a football helmet, he dropped to 17th of the 20 entries; proving that if at first you don't succeed, don't try again.

Two Italian superstars both failed to win Eurovision. Iva Zanicchi and Domenico Modugno embrace – in consolation?

ITALIAN STALLION

Domenico Modugno stumped up for Italy in both 1958 and 1959, but couldn't persuade the judges of either contest he had the best song, despite the record-buying public clearly disagreeing. **Michèle Arnaud** for Luxembourg sang their first songs in 1956, the only year two songs per country were allowed. Since we don't know the results from the inaugural contest, we've no way of knowing if singing twice in one contest is a good idea or not. Probably not. **Esther Hart** considered trying it in 2003 when she entered both the UK and Dutch heats. She won the Dutch, so withdrew from the British. Had she not done so, maybe that ghastly, humiliating UK "nul points" in 2003 could have been avoided.

Making her 2nd consecutive appearance for Germany in 1958, Margot Hielscher was Eurovision's first entrant to use props during her performance.

ON THE LINE

Margot Hielscher was assured of a warm welcome on home ground in 1957 when she sang 'Telefon, Telefon' ('Telephone, Telephone') in Frankfurt, complete with the contest's first ever prop. Placing 4th was a good result, so naturally encouraged, she returned in 1958 with 'Für Zwei Groschen Musik' ('Music For Two'), dressed as a beauty queen and clutching a handful of 7" vinyl singles, which she "played" on an imaginary record player. Maybe it was too early in its day for Eurovision props and gimmicks and Margot slipped back to 7th and gave Eurovision up.

THINGS CAN ONLY GET BETTER?

Tony Wegas also tried his hand back-to-back for the Austrians and did reasonably well in 1992 with 'Zusammen Geh'n' ('Together Straight'), although as one of the pre-contest favourites, 10th was actually fairly disappointing. Tony switched from a ballad to an upbeat rock number for 1993's 'Maria Magdalena' and brought along **Gary Lux** as a backing singer, but things got worse for Tony and he fell back to 14th. Things then got even worse when he was jailed for a series of violent thefts and thus three contests in a row proved impossible.

FIRST TO LAST

Estonia's Eurovision debut was woefully unsuccessful, but in 1996, **Maarja-Liis Ilus** teamed up with **Ivo Linna** to salvage national pride and 'Kaelakee Hääl' ('Voice Of The Necklace') placed 5th in Oslo. Flushed with this huge improvement in their fortunes, Maarja-Liis was immediately sent straight back to the contest, this time alone and under the wing of a global recording contract. 'Keelatud Maa' ('Hold On To Love') didn't score quite so well and the release of her English album *First In Line* didn't spark the global popularity expected.

TWO FOR TWO

Arguably Germany's two most successful contest participants both made it two in a row, with **Katja Ebstein** placing 3rd in 1970 and 1971, Germany's best placing yet. **Lena Meyer-Landrut** went further to win in 2010 and scored a massive 246 points to triumph, immediately declaring she'd be back to win again in 2011. Alas, the judges didn't agree it was such a great plan and 'Taken By A Stranger' pulled up in 10th place.

MAKING AN IMPRESSION

Moira & Chris came to Millstreet to sing backing vocals for **William Mangion** in 1993 and left such an impression that they were singing for Malta alone in Dublin one year later. By coming out of Mangion's shadow, they did themselves a huge favour and moved up from 8th to 5th with 'More Than Love'.

SUMMER LOVE

Nora Brockstedt sang Norway's debut entry in 1960 'Voi Voi' ('Hey Hey') and scored 4th – which was, perhaps unbelievably, Norway's second best result until they won in 1985. Not knowing what future agony lay ahead, Nora returned in 1961 and slipped downwards to 7th with 'Sommer I Palma' ('Summer In Palma').

Norway's Anne Karine Strøm earns the first of her record two last place finishes.

THE NOT-QUITE-PERFECT STRØM

From 1973 to 1976 it was **The Bendik Singers** who tried hard to improve Norway's fortunes. As a unit, they combined for 7th place in 1973, but when **Anne Karine Strøm** was promoted to lead singer in 1974 with her colleagues as her backing group, they slumped to joint last. Maybe miffed that Anne Karine got top billing, **Ellen Nickolaysen** left the Bendiks and tried her hand as a soloist too, placing 18th in 1975 of the 19 songs in Stockholm. Not to be outdone, Anne Karine went solo too and placed last all alone in 1976. The group's mentor, **Arne Bendikson**, had marginally more success when he sang for Norway in 1964, placing 8th. Clearly the Bendik touch wasn't what Norway needed, but it took them an age to figure that out.

RECORD BREAKER

Technically, **Lys Assia** could claim an all-time record of four straight Eurovision entries. Alas, since she sang two songs in 1956 before returning in 1957 and 1958, she can only boast joint status as a Eurovision "threepeater". Ms. Lys can, however, claim to be the only singer to perform in three straight contests in three different languages. Not that she needs another claim to Eurovision fame. Being the first winner puts her into every history book, every time.

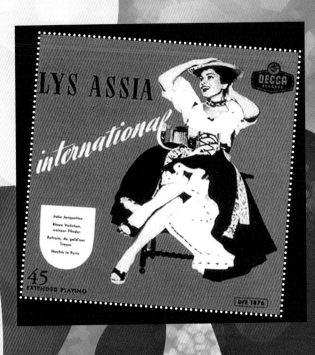

SPAIN'S SUCCESS

Spain's **Raphael** made his two Eurovision appearances in two consecutive contests and both times scored Spain's best successes to date. His 'Yo Soy Aquél' ('I'm That One') placed 7th in 1966 and 'Hablemos Del Amor' ('Words Of Love') improved to 6th in 1967. He'd clearly paved the way for Spain in the contest as he retired from competing, yet stood aside to watch Spain win back-to-back contests in 1968 and 1969. These things must surely hurt.

RING A DING RON

Ronnie Carroll is the sole Brit to sing at two Eurovisions in a row and he achieved the same result both times. In Luxembourg 1962, he sang the inane 'Ring-A-Ding Girl' to achieve joint 4th and then on home ground in 1963, opened the show with another 4th-placed effort, 'Say Wonderful Things'. At the climax of the 1963 edition, as the home artist, he was asked to present **Grethe & Jørgen Ingmann** with flowers for their victory. Had he won himself, who would have handed over his own floral tribute?

Britain's "Little Minstrel" Ronnie Carroll appeared in 1962 and 1963, finishing 4th on both occasions.

Rock And Roll Kids

EUROVISION'S OLDEST AND YOUNGEST

The Eurovision Song Contest welcomes entries of all ages. From Russian grannies to performers barely out of nappies, all have a chance to shine on Europe's greatest stage.

The Buranovskiye Babushki placed 2nd for Russia in 2011, and went home with their church coffers replenished.

AGE IS BUT A NUMBER

Until 2008, 56-year-old **Lale Andersen** was Eurovision's oldest performer. She was outstripped by almost 20 years in 2008, when a 75-year-old Croatian, **75 Cents**, teamed up with **Kraljevi Ulice** to earn 21st place in Belgrade with *'Romanca'* *('Romance')*. 75 Cents was a mere youngster compared to who was to follow. Even 76-year-old **Engelbert Humperdinck** was denied the record when he entered the contest for the UK in 2012.

SUPER SEPTUAGENARIANS

Briefly, a group of grannies from central Russia held the record for being Eurovision's oldest participants. **Buranovskiye Babuskhi**, the sextet of septuagenarians, had attempted to represent Russia at Eurovision two years before, ending 2nd in the domestic heat. Their story of forming a choir and entering Eurovision merely to fund their local church eventually won international recognition and next time around, their song 'Party For Everybody' easily won their national contest and headed to Baku as the firm favourite. There the grannies finished 2nd, a long way behind the Swedish victor and they returned to their church, doubtless with their coffers suitably replenished thanks to their sugary-sweet, fizzy sponsor.

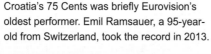

Croatia's 75 Cents was briefly Eurovision's oldest performer. Emil Ramsauer, a 95-year-old from Switzerland, took the record in 2013.

COMING OF AGE

Sandra Kim, the Belgian singer of Italian ancestry, represented French-speaking Belgium in 1986, claiming to be 15 years old when she performed 'J'Aime La Vie' ('I Love Life') in Bergen. She even stated her age in the song's lyric. However, all was not what it seemed and it later emerged that young Sandra was even younger. She was only 13 years of age. The deception led to Swiss TV (whose song had placed 2nd) petitioning for her disqualification, but to no avail. Sandra retained her title and, under current contest rules, will always retain her record of youngest ever winner.

SWEET SIXTEEN

The Junior Eurovision Song Contest launched in 2003, to allow performers under the age of sixteen a chance to develop their singing and songwriting skills. Prior to 1990, Eurovision had not had any lower (or upper) age limit. Until **Sandra Kim**'s victory in 1986, **Gigliola Cinquetti** had been the contest's youngest champion, aged 16 in 1964.

TWIN WIN

At just 9 years old, twins **Anastasiya** and **Maria Tolmacheva** scored Russia's first ever Eurovision victory in 2006, albeit in the Junior version of the contest. So perhaps it was no surprise when Russian TV then chose the twins to represent them at the 2014 contest in Copenhagen at the age of 17, under the wing of **Alla Pugacheva** and latterly her ex-husband **Philip Kirkorov**. **The Tolmachevy Sisters** performed 'Shine' in the contest, appearing during the height of the civil conflict with neighbouring Ukraine. The 10,000-strong audience showed Russia their disapproval by booing their qualification for the final, which didn't seem to stop the girls shining through their smiles.

With the help of their quiffs, Ireland's Jedward peaked in 8th place in 2011 and earned the record for tallest hair.

THE X FACTOR

Lea Bundgaard is possibly Eurovision's youngest ever performer, joining Dad Søren's group **Hot Eyes** in Gothenburg for Denmark in 1985 only to place 11th. Although not technically seen, **Hot Eyes' Kirsten Siggard** may have been accompanied on stage by Eurovision's youngest ever entrant, being heavily pregnant when she appeared in both 1984 and 1988. It's quite possible that Spanish quartet **Javier Glaria**, **Alexis Carmona**, **Beatriz Carmona** and **Rosalía Rodríguez**, may be Eurovision's youngest ever entrants as backing singers for **Betty Missiego** in 1979. Alas, history has not recorded their ages at the time, but they were certainly all pre-pubescent.

Lady, Lady

EUROVISION'S WINNING FEMALE WRITERS

If you compiled a list of Eurovision's competing or winning singers and another of the contest's hosts, it would be quicker to count the men than the women. A lot quicker. However, those are probably the only tally's where the ladies would outnumber the gentlemen.

SELF COMPOSED

Claude Morgan became the first woman to compose the music for a Eurovision winner in 1973, when teamed with lyrics from **Vline Buggy**, and **Anne-Marie David** triumphed for Luxembourg on home ground with 'Tu Te Reconnaîtras' ('You'll Recognize Yourself'). Claude didn't apparently inspire other lady composers to step forward and those who did weren't at all successful for another five years.

A TOUCH OF FROST

Julie Frost wasn't the first American to win Eurovision (that record already passed to singer **Katrina Leskanich**), but she was the first American to write a Eurovision winner, penning both music and lyrics in partnership with Dane **John Gordon** for Germany. Their song 'Satellite' for **Lena Meyer-Landrut** topped the charts in six countries and was certified platinum at home where the track sold in excess of 600,000 copies, later picking up the 2010 Krone Music Award for Best Single.

In 1973 Anne-Marie David scored 129 of a possible 160 (80.63%); the highest score ever.

EQUAL WRITES

In most respects, writing Eurovision winners has been a man's world. It wasn't until the 14th contest that a woman penned the winning song for the first time, when **Lenny Kuhr** wrote the lyrics for her own song 'De Troubadour' ('The Troubadour'). Lenny wrote herself into the record book with half the writing credits for a fourth of the winners. Since she actually appeared on stage with an uncredited male guitarist, maybe it was only half a performance, too.

TEAM SWEDE

Sweden's **Sandra Bjurman** went one better than **Britt Lindeborg** by not only penning the lyrics to a winner, but also co-composing the music for Azerbaijan's winning song 'Running Scared' in 2011. For this win, she teamed up with another Swede **Stefan Örn** and British writer **Ian Farquharson**. Sandra (together with Örn) had written the previous year's 'Drip Drop' for the Azeris, which had been widely tipped to win in Oslo, but had finished 6th. *'Running Scared'* was chosen from around 70 submissions to AiTV and the singers **Ell/Nikki** (**Eldar Gasimov** and **Nigar Jamal**) were chosen from a long-running televised talent show. They never worked together on new material again.

2013 – LUCKY YEAR FOR LADIES

For the first time in 2013, two ladies got their names etched on the Grand Prix when **Lise Cabble** and **Julia Fabrin Jakobsen** teamed up with **Thomas Stengaard** to co-write and compose 'Only Teardrops' for **Emmelie De Forest** and scored Denmark's third Eurovision victory. Outside of Denmark, where the winning single achieved platinum sales status, the track was also a huge hit in Greece, Brazil, Sweden, Ukraine, Spain, Germany, Luxembourg and Finland.

Denmark's third victory came in 2013, when Emmelie de Forrest became the contest's second barefoot winner.

When?

SINGERS WHO HAVE KEPT ON TRYING

If at first you don't succeed, try, try and try again. A maxim that many Eurovision singers have applied with relish over the 60 years of the contest.

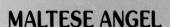

Chiara became a Maltese national hero when she placed 3rd in 1998.

MALTESE ANGEL

Malta's **Chiara** became a national heroine in 1998 when she placed 3rd at the contest in Birmingham. A rank outsider for the competition with 'The One That I Love', Chiara had impressed enormously with her powerful vocal of the song, entirely alone on stage and appeared to be heading for a win. On the very last vote from FYR Macedonia, she dropped from 1st to 3rd, yet at least 7,000 fans descended on Valletta airport to welcome her home. She came back to the 50th contest in Kyiv, 2005 and moved up a place with her song 'Angel', which she penned herself, and tried one last shot at the title in Moscow, 2009. This time, 'What If We…?' was not what the judges were looking for and she placed 22nd of the 25 entries.

SAVE THE BEST FOR LAST

Anne Karine Strøm is the only singer ever to have finished last twice. Anne Karine actually got off to a respectable start in the contest, finishing 7th in 1973 as part of the group **The Bendik Singers**, singing 'It's Just A Game'. Clearly encouraged, Anne took centre billing the following year in Brighton, only to end up in joint last place with 'The First Day Of Love'. Undeterred, Anne came back alone two years later with her song 'Mata Hari', only to take last place all on her own. She never showed her face in the contest again.

SHEER WILL POWER

British singer **Ireen Sheer** has made three attempts to win Eurovision, for both Luxembourg and Germany. Her first entry, 'Bye, Bye, I Love You', was naturally sung in French for the Grand Duchy in 1974. Finishing joint 4th, Ireen was much lampooned for her English accent in her French vocal. Her accent burst through again in 1978 when she represented Germany in Paris with 'Feuer' ('Fire'), dropping down the field to 7th. Not getting the hint, Ireen was back for Luxembourg again in 1985, this time in the company of Dutch singer **Margo**, Frenchman **Franck Olivier**, German **Chris Roberts**, Canadian **Diane Solomon** and Englishman **Malcolm Roberts** to perform a **Ralph Siegel** song 'Kinder, Children, Enfants'. They placed 13th, far behind Britain's own 4th-placed effort.

British singer Ireen Sheer sang in French in 1974 and German in 1978. Neither proved successful.

WHICH SINGERS COMPETED THE MOST OFTEN?
ONLY SINGERS WHO HAVE BEEN MEMBERS OF GROUPS OR
WHO WERE GIVEN CREDIT FOR A PERFORMANCE ARE INCLUDED.
UNCREDITED APPEARANCES AS BACKING SINGERS ARE EXCLUDED.

LYS ASSIA	4	SWITZERLAND 56 (x2), 57, 58
FUD LECLERC	4	BELGIUM 56, 58, 60, 62
ELISABETH ANDREASSEN	4	SWEDEN 82*, NORWAY 85*, 94*, 96
PETER, SUE AND MARC	4	SWITZERLAND, 71, 76, 79*, 81
CORRY BROKKEN	3	THE NETHERLANDS 56, 57, 58
HANNE KROGH	3	NORWAY 71, 85*, 91*
DOMENICO MODUGNO	3	ITALY 58, 59, 66
HOT EYES	3	DENMARK 84, 85, 88
IREEN SHEER	3	LUXEMBOURG 74, 85*, GERMANY 78
ANITA SKORGAN^	3	NORWAY 77, 79, 82*
JAHN TEIGEN	3	NORWAY 78, 82*, 83
KATJA EBSTEIN	3	GERMANY 70, 71, 80
STELLA	3	THE NETHERLANDS 70*, BELGIUM 77*, 82
KIRSTI SPARBOE	3	NORWAY 65, 67, 69
ROMUALD	3	MONACO 64, 74 LUXEMBOURG 69
SANDRA REEMER^	3	THE NETHERLANDS 72*, 76, 79*
MARIE BERGMAN	3	SWEDEN 71*, 72*, 94*
ANNE KARINE STRØM	3	NORWAY 73*, 74, 76
TOMMY SEEBACH	3	DENMARK 79, 81*, 93*
UDO JÜRGENS	3	AUSTRIA 64, 65, 66
ANNA VISSI (VISHY)	3	GREECE 80, 06, CYPRUS 82
GARY LUX^	3	AUSTRIA 83*, 85, 87
CAROLA	3	SWEDEN 83, 91, 06
WIND	3	GERMANY 85, 87, 92
CONSTANTINOS	3	CYPRUS 96, 02*, 05
CHIARA	3	MALTA 98, 05, 09

* AS PART OF A GROUP OR DUET.
^ ALSO UNCREDITED BACKING SINGER ON OTHER OCCASIONS.
EVRIDIKI REPRESENTED CYPRUS IN 92 AND 94 BUT FAILED TO SURVIVE THE 07 QUALIFIER.
EIRIKUR HAUKSSON REPRESENTED ICELAND AS PART OF ICY IN 86 AND NORWAY AS PART OF JUST 4 FUN IN 91, BUT FAILED
TO QUALIFY AS A SOLOIST FOR ICELAND IN 2007.
VALENTINA MONETTA REPRESENTED SAN MARINO IN BOTH THE 2012 AND 2013 CONTESTS, BUT FAILED TO QUALIFY ON BOTH
OCCASIONS, BEFORE REACHING THE FINAL IN 2014

FRIENDS, WHO REPRESENTED SWEDEN IN 2001, ARE NO RELATION TO THE THREE COMPLETELY SEPARATE BACKING GROUPS
THAT ACCOMPANIED FINLAND 1976, GREECE 2010 & RUSSIA 2010.
THE NINA WHO REPRESENTED SPAIN IN 1989 IS NOT THE SAME NINA WHO SANG FOR SERBIA IN 2011.
THE EMMA WHO REPRESENTED THE UK IN 1990 IS NOT THE SAME EMMA WHO SANG FOR ITALY IN 2014.

SINGERS WHO REPRESENTED MULTIPLE COUNTRIES

JEAN PHILIPPE	FRANCE 59, SWITZERLAND 62
SIW MALMKVIST	SWEDEN 60, GERMANY 69
ROMUALD	MONACO 64, 74, LUXEMBOURG 69
TEREZA	MONACO 66, YUGOSLAVIA 72
MICHÈLE TORR	LUXEMBOURG 66, MONACO 77
STELLA	THE NETHERLANDS 70*, BELGIUM 77*, 82
ANNE-MARIE DAVID	LUXEMBOURG 73, FRANCE 79
IREEN SHEER	LUXEMBOURG 74, 85*, GERMANY 78
ELPIDA	GREECE 78, CYPRUS 86
ANNA VISSI (VISHY)	GREECE 80, 06, CYPRUS 82
ELISABETH ANDREASSEN	SWEDEN 82*, NORWAY 85*, 94*, 96
EIRIKUR HAUKSSON~	ICELAND 86*, NORWAY 91*
DORIS (DRAGOVIĆ)	YUGOSLAVIA 86, CROATIA 99
ŽELJKO JOKSIMOVIĆ ◊	SERBIA & MONTENEGRO 04, SERBIA 12

~ ALSO REPRESENTED ICELAND IN THE 2007 SEMI-FINAL, BUT FAILED TO QUALIFY.
◊ ALSO WROTE THE 2003 ENTRY FOR BOSNIA-HERZEGOVINA.

NUL POINTS ANITA

Anita Skorgan kept her Eurovision dream alive in the face of all sensible opinion. She caused the BBC a headache in 1977, when Norwegian broadcaster NRK had been so shocked at the way the 18-year-old was portrayed in the planned postcard to introduce her song 'Casanova', they all had to be abandoned, and she limped in to 15th place. Coming back in 1979, she did slightly better with 'Oliver' to rise to 11th, Norway's best showing since 1973! 1981 saw her as a backing vocalist for **Finn Kalvik** in Dublin as he scored a resounding zero, so naturally she teamed up with Norway's other "nul pointer" **Jahn Teigen** for 'Adieu' in 1982. Harrogate was emblazoned with stickers and posters pleading "Vote For Norway" and Anita and Teigen got enough points to register 12th. She came back with Teigen in 1983 (now her husband) and supported him on backing vocals as he scored 9th place with 'Do Re Mi'. Skorgan's best Eurovision, however, came when she wasn't on stage at all. Returning to Dublin in 1988, she wrote 'For Vår Joord' ('For Your Love'), sung by **Karoline Krüger** and achieved 5th place.

Norway's Anita Skorgan kept on trying and trying as a singer, but got her best result in 1988 as a composer.

Norway's record-breaking third "nul points" came courtesy of Finn Kalvik in 1981, when his ABBA-produced track 'Aldri I Livet' ('Never In My Life') failed to score in Dublin.

## CHAPTER TWO

Nul Points

With unexpected onstage invaders, perilous
live performances and plain old bad luck,
Eurovision proves, year after year, that it
isn't just scoring the dreaded "nul points"
that has struck fear into the
hearts of entrants.

Rock Bottom

A HISTORY OF "NUL POINTS"

The era of "nul points" began in 1962, when four nations failed to score a single point in Luxembourg. By dint of the running order, Belgium have the ignominy of Eurovision's first zero, but Spain, Austria and the Netherlands were regarded as equally awful.

JUST SAY NUL

The Nordic nations joined the "nul points" club in 1963 when Norway, Sweden and Finland (together with the Dutch) all failed to win over a single jury at TV Centre in London. Ironically as it turned out, this was the year the first nation from the region took home gold, with Denmark winning out thanks to help from the struggling Norwegians.

THE FAMOUS FOUR

The number of "nul pointers" remained at four in 1965, but the wooden spoon was shared between four nations who'd suffered the ignominy before. Spain, Finland, Belgium and Germany were all equally humiliated, but in the case of the Belgians and Germans, it would be the last such ridicule.

In 1982, Kojo earned Finland its third "nul points" with a song translated as 'Bomb Out'. It certainly did.

THE LAST NUL

The last "nul points" achieved before the "douze points" scoring system was introduced in 1975 was Luxembourg's 1970 effort 'Je Suis Tombé Du Ciel' ('I Fell From The Sky') from **David Alexandre Winter**. He was a pretty big name at the time, and his humiliation came on stage in Amsterdam in what many predicted would be the last Eurovision Song Contest. Thankfully for David, the show went from strength to strength, or it could have been much worse for the Dutch born singer in the history books.

WORST OF ALL

The year after Norway got their third "nul points", Finland achieved their third. 'Nuku Pomiin' ('Oversleep') was aptly titled as **Kojo** slumped to the bottom of the Harrogate entry list, probably to nobody's real surprise. A year later in 1983, both Spain and Turkey shared the dishonours, the first time since 1966 the juries hadn't been able to decide which of the songs was truly the worst of all.

NO HOPE FOR NORWAY

Norway cemented their reputation as Eurovision's most hopeless nation when they scored a hat-trick of zeroes in Dublin, 1981. What made **Finn Kalvik**'s spectacular failure even more embarrassing was that the recording of his entry 'Aldri I Livet' ('Never In My Life') was produced by **Benny Andersson** and **Björn Ulvæus**, with backing vocals from **Anni-Frid Lyngstad**. Clearly **ABBA**'s magic touch didn't translate across the border and Finn returned home a national laughing stock.

ZERO TO HERO

Two nations were deemed worthy of no points in 1966: Monaco and, perhaps astonishingly, Italy. The Italians were represented by **Domenico Modugno,** Eurovision's biggest-selling artist to date, singing the San Remo Song Festival winner 'Dio, Come To Amo' ('God, How I Love You'), which went on to be a huge hit for former winner **Gigliola Cinquetti**. Shows how much the judges knew about a hit.

POOR TURKEYS

Cetin Alp & The Short Waves' 'Opera' failed to score for Turkey in 1983, but the next few years were "nul points" free. Then Turkey got back into the groove with **Seyyal Tanner**'s 'Şarkim Sevgi Üstüne' ('This Melody'). A huge movie and singing star in Turkey, Ms. Tanner and her group **Locomotif** were astonished to find their predictions of a first Turkish victory way, way off the mark. Still, Seyyal knew where the blame lay and placed it firmly on the shoulders of the orchestra's conductor, **Garo Mafyan**. His reply isn't recorded.

NUL WAY NORWAY!

Norway set a new "nul points" record in 1997, when their fourth entry to fail to score propped up the bottom of the scoreboard, albeit in partnership with Portugal. The following year, the Swiss almost caught up, achieving their third blank register.

RED-FACED REPUBLIC

Although not strictly finalists, both Switzerland and the Czech Republic have been drubbed in the semi-finals, with **Piero & The MusicStars** totally humiliated in the 2004 semi, leaving them nothing to 'Celebrate' at all. Since the Czechs were bounced out without a point in the 2009 semi with **Gypsy.cz**'s 'Aven Romale' ('Come In Gypsies'), the Republic stayed away until the 60th contest in 2015.

In 2004, Switzerland's Piero & The MusicStars had nothing to 'Celebrate', becoming the first nation to score zero in a semi-final.

GROUND ZERO

After 1991, the next two contests were zero-free, but in 1994, Lithuania swept all before them to join Portugal as the only other nation to achieve a resounding zero from the juries on their debut. 'Lopšinė Mylimai' ('Sweetheart's Lullaby') was a very morbid piece, performed in Dublin by the aggressive looking **Ovidijus Vyšniauskas**. Such was the agony, Lithuania weren't seen in Eurovision again for another five years.

MOST TIMES SCORED "NUL POINTS"
(EXCLUDES THE 1956 CONTEST & NON-QUALIFYING SONGS)

NORWAY	4	63, 78, 81, 97
AUSTRIA	3	62, 88, 91
FINLAND	3	62, 65, 82
SPAIN	3	62, 65, 83
SWITZERLAND*	3	64, 67, 98
THE NETHERLANDS	2	62, 63
BELGIUM	2	62, 65
GERMANY	2	64, 65
PORTUGAL	2	64, 97
TURKEY	2	83, 87

*SWITZERLAND ALSO SCORED 0 IN THE 2004 SEMI-FINAL

JEMINI CRASH LAND

When the contest expanded to 26 nations in 2003, the unthinkable happened: the United Kingdom, arguably Europe's leading pop nation and statistically Eurovision's most successful country, was humiliated by the other 25 participants when **Jemini**'s off-key performance of 'Cry Baby' left the country in tears. No song in the Eurovision final has failed to score since, and so in the expanded competition Jemini maintain the record for the lowest-scoring song in Eurovision history. A reason to cry, for sure.

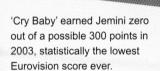

'Cry Baby' earned Jemini zero out of a possible 300 points in 2003, statistically the lowest Eurovision score ever.

THE NUL POINTERS!

1962	BELGIUM	'Ton Nom'
1962	SPAIN	'Llámame'
1962	GERMANY	'Nur In Der Wiener Luft'
1962	NETHERLANDS	'Katinka'
1963	NETHERLANDS	'Een Speeldoos'
1963	NORWAY	'Solherv'
1963	FINLAND	'Muistejeni Laulu'
1963	SWEDEN	'En Gång I Stockholm'
1964	GERMANY	'Man Gewöhnt Sich So Schnell An Das Schöne'
1964	PORTUGAL	'Oração'
1964	YUGOSLAVIA	'Život Je Sklopio Krug'
1964	SWITZERLAND	'I Miei Pensieri'
1965	SPAIN	'Qué Bueno, Qué Bueno'
1965	GERMANY	'Paradies, Wo Bist Du?'
1965	BELGIUM	'Als Het Weer Lente Is'
1965	FINLAND	'Aurinko Laskee Länteen'
1966	MONACO	'Bien Plus Fort'
1966	ITALY	'Dio, Come Te Amo'
1967	SWITZERLAND	'Quel Cœur Vas-Tu Briser?'
1978	NORWAY	'Mil Etter Mil"
1981	NORWAY	'Aldri I Livet'
1982	FINLAND	'Nuku Pommiin'
1983	SPAIN	'Quién Maneja Mi Barca'
1983	TURKEY	'Opera'
1987	TURKEY	'Šarkim Sevgi Üstüne'
1988	AUSTRIA	'Lisa, Mona Lisa'
1989	ICELAND	'Það Sem Enginn Sér'
1991	AUSTRIA	'Venedig Im Regen'
1994	LITHUANIA	'Lopšin Mylimai'
1997	NORWAY	'San Francisco'
1997	PORTUGAL	'Antes Do Adeus'
1998	SWITZERLAND	'Lass' Ihn'
2003	UNITED KINGDOM	'Cry Baby'

IN 2004, SWITZERLAND'S 'CELEBRATE' SCORED 'NUL POINTS' IN THE SEMI-FINAL, AS DID THE CZECH REPUBLIC'S 'AVEN ROMALE' IN 2009.

Should've Known Better

THE COMEBACK STARS WHO SHOULD HAVE STAYED AWAY

Eurovision has seen established stars take part hoping to elevate their careers. Alas, for many, they've seen it as a last chance to recapture former glories and in that instance, it's never proved very successful.

CRINKLY BOTTOM

As recently as 2012, legendary crooner **Engelbert Humperdinck** represented the UK with 'Love Will Set You Free', hoping to rekindle his former hit-making career. Although the contest did give him his first (albeit minor) UK hit since 1973, he was all but one place off the bottom of the scoreboard.

At 76, Engelbert Humperdinck, "the King of Romance", probably left his Eurovision run a tad late in his career.

NOT-SO PLASTIC FANTASTIC

In the late 1970s **Plastic Bertrand** was briefly the world's most famous Belgian when he took his punk hit 'Ça Plane Pour Moi' ('All's Good For Me') up the charts all around Europe and beyond. Alas for Plastic, it soon transpired his voice wasn't the one heard on the track and although he toured Europe, Australia, Japan and North America on the back of the track's success, he soon disappeared under a mire of legal issues. When Luxembourg came knocking in 1987, Plastic leapt at the chance of a comeback, but sadly 'Amour, Amour' ('Love, Love') placed 21st of the 22 songs in Brussels 1987 and he hasn't been heard much of since.

Belgian Plastic Bertrand treasures the gold disc he earned in 1978, despite not singing on the hit that bore his name. His 1987 Eurovision song was equally disastrous.

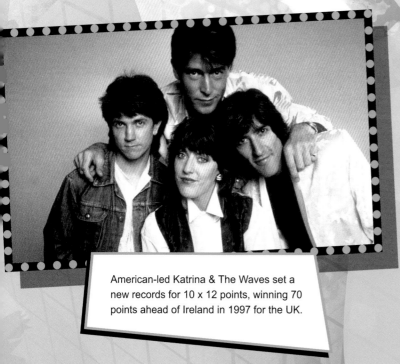

American-led Katrina & The Waves set a new records for 10 x 12 points, winning 70 points ahead of Ireland in 1997 for the UK.

NO LONGER MAKING WAVES

Anglo-American rockers **Katrina & The Waves** had enjoyed pan-global success in the mid 1980s with the classic track 'Walking On Sunshine'. Although often referred to stateside as a "one hit wonder", the band had further successes in various countries in the immediate aftermath, but by the time they took part in the *Great British Song Contest* in 1997, they were largely relegated to minor gigs and festivals. Their emphatic win with 'Love Shine A Light' in Dublin could have relaunched them, but despite the huge hit that ensued, rivalries in the band led to an acrimonious split within weeks of their win, and no further successes.

DISAPPEARING ACT

German girl group **No Angels** had been enormously successful since coming to the fore in 2000 as the winners of Germany's successful talent show *Popstars*, with the quintet already hailed as the biggest-selling German girl band and the most successful European girl group, even outselling the British **Spice Girls**. Multiple awards matched the multiple chart toppers, but by 2003 the group had disbanded to pursue solo projects. In 2007 the girls reformed as a quartet and released another successful album, paving the way to their victory in the domestic Eurovision qualifier. At the final in Belgrade 2008, the Bulgarian voters picked 'Disappear' as the best song of the night – the first "douze points" for Germany since 2004 – but there was scant support from any other nation and they soon disappeared once more.

Having outsold the Spice Girls, Germany's No Angels reunited in 2008 but found their girl power had evaporated.

SCOOCH OVER

British band **Scooch** briefly enjoyed considerable success from 1999, having won a TV talent show, and began to score hits in the UK and Japan. They scored their last hit in 2000 and seemed to have largely disappeared other than for some reality TV appearances. In 2007, they returned and controversially won through the BBC's heat to sing 'Flying The Flag' for Britain in Helsinki and the track gave them the biggest hit of their career to date. Alas, it proved a false reboot and 23rd place with scores from only Malta and Ireland left the group embarrassed and unable to capitalize on further commercial success.

WET WET WET

Although you won't find their name anywhere in the Eurovision archives, **The Weather Girls** attempted a comeback of sorts by entering Germany's domestic final in 2002. Decades on from the global smash 'It's Raining Men', the girls were reformed by one half of the original duo, **Izora Armstead**, and her daughter, but their song 'Get Up' failed to win through to Tallinn and the hoped-for reboot never came.

The innuendo laden 'Flying The Flag' crash-landed in Helsinki for Britain's Scooch, yet earned them the biggest hit of their career.

BELIEVE IN ME

Bonnie Tyler had been a global hit maker for many years from the late 1970s, topping the charts in Europe, Asia and North America, where she found considerable fame and fortune. At the height of her success in 1984, the BBC invited her to represent the UK in the 1985 contest, but she was too heavily committed internationally for the schedule. By the time they asked again in 2013, Bonnie's diary was considerably lighter and she went to Malmö with 'Believe In Me'. The comeback failed and Bonnie returned to touring Europe to dwindling audiences.

FEELING BLUE

Boy band **Blue** followed **The Shadows**' lead and reformed in 2011 specifically to represent the UK at Eurovision with 'I Can'. The song fell well short of expectations with both the judges and the record-buying public and although an album followed in 2013, the lads have largely been dormant since, failing to recreate their chart-topping successes of the early new millennium.

INTERNATIONAL STYLE

Israel's **Dana International** made a huge impact on the world's media when she first tried to represent her nation at Eurovision in 1995 with 'Layla Tov, Eropa' ('Good Night, Europe') but she wasn't selected to go to Dublin. When she did get the ticket to Birmingham in 1998, the global interest was frenzied at the thought of a transsexual artist taking part and world success seemed assured when she scored her victory with 'Diva'. Alas, although the media continued to be very interested, the music-buying public were not. Dana returned to Eurovision as a writer in 2008 with 'The Fire In Your Eyes' for **Boaz Mauda**, which placed 9th in Belgrade, and then with her own song 'Ding Dong' in Düsseldorf 2011. The voters dumped her out in the semi-finals and Dana took a two-year career break. Her return hasn't reignited the fires as yet.

Don't Play That Song Again

DISASTERS AND MISHAPS

Technical woes have beleaguered Eurovision since its earliest days. Hardly surprisingly really, when considering the enormous complexity of the operation in hand.

TECHNICAL KNOCKOUT

In 1958, Italy performed first in the contest in Hilversum and in 1958, Italy performed last in the contest in Hilversum. Really. **Domenico Modugno** sang his song 'Nel Blu Di Pinto Di Blue' ('In The Sky, Painted Blue') to rousing applause. After Switzerland had apparently closed the contest, hostess **Hannie Lips** made her entrance, presumably to commence moderating the scoring. Instead, she announced that audio difficulties in several nations had meant they'd missed the Italian song altogether. As a result, Italy would get to sing again. It's one of only four songs to be performed twice that didn't win the competition.

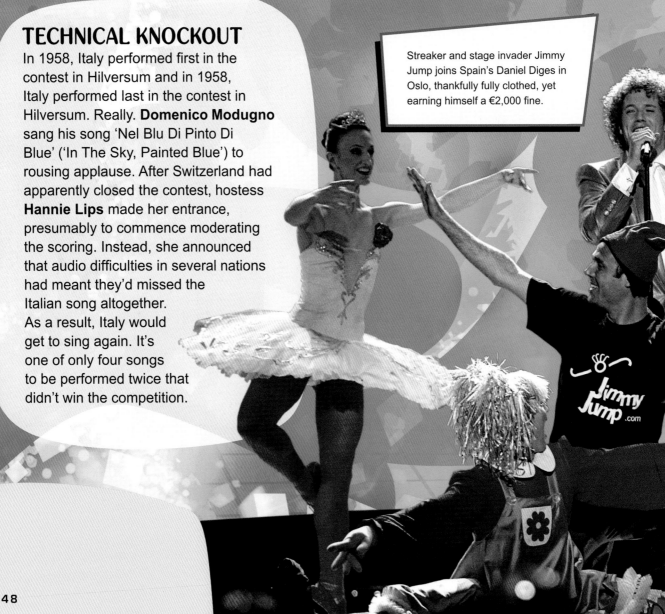

Streaker and stage invader Jimmy Jump joins Spain's Daniel Diges in Oslo, thankfully fully clothed, yet earning himself a €2,000 fine.

STAGE INVASION

Professional stage invader **Jimmy Jump** saw his opportunity to become Europe's newest celebrity in 2010 during Spain's performance in Oslo. Alas, he may not have made the wisest choice for his moment in the spotlight. **Daniel Diges** was singing 'Algo Pequeñito' ('Something Tiny') in the cursed second position in the running order, when somewhat tiny Jimmy leapt onto the stage in his red hat. Alas, there were already five fairly ludicrously dressed circus performers on stage with Daniel and most viewers never noticed Jimmy suddenly in amongst them. Security officers certainly did and as the director cut to wide shots of the audience, black clad guards chased Jimmy off the stage and into custody. Some fans suggest it was all pre-arranged, as Spain had drawn the death slot in the running order, and hint that singing again at the end of the presentation might have helped Daniel score 15th place. But perhaps not.

BACKING TRACK CHAOS PT. 1

Spain opened the 1990 contest in Zagreb with sister duo **Azúcar Moreno** singing 'Bandido' ('Bandit') first to an expectant audience of (so the hosts stated) 1,000 million viewers. Unfortunately, conductor **Eduardo Leiva** couldn't hear that the backing track had started and he didn't cue the live orchestra. The girls were already on stage, getting in to their groove when they realized something was amiss with the music and totally confused, quickly left again. They recovered brilliantly to earn 5th place, but Spain's TVE refused to use backing tracks for many subsequent years.

BACKING TRACK CHAOS PT. 2

RTÉ gained a reputation for producing Eurovisions of high quality. They've certainly had enough practice. Yet in 1988, during the presentation of Germany's entry 'Lied Für Einen Freund' ('Song For A Friend') from mother and daughter combo **Maxi & Chris Garden,** things didn't go to plan. At 14, Maxi was hoping to become Eurovision's second youngest-ever winner and they were installed as the bookies' favourite. Alas, the pre-recorded backing track supplied by writers **Ralph Siegel & Bernd Meinunger** cut out during the song's performance. The RTÉ Concert Orchestra directed by **Mike Thatcher** kept playing, but the sound was distinctly different. ARD requested to sing again, but to no avail. The 14-year-old Maxi had to settle for 14th place.

In 1959, Britain's Pearl Carr & Teddy Johnson became the first husband-and-wife team to sing at Eurovision and the first of 15 UK entrants to place 2nd.

LAST MINUTE REPRISE

In 1959, French hosts ORTF made a supremely generous gesture to the competing nations by inviting both the 2nd and 3rd placed entries to reprise their songs at the end of the contest. After Dutch winner **Teddie Scholten** accepted the Grand Prix and sung 'Een Beetje' ('A Little') again, both the UK's **Pearl Carr & Teddy Johnson** and France's own **Jean Philippe** took to the revolving set to perform their respective entries once more. As the clock was already fast approaching or was way beyond midnight in most of the viewing nations, it was decided never to extend such courtesy in the future. However, Ireland did confer flowers on the 2nd and 3rd placed artists in 1971.

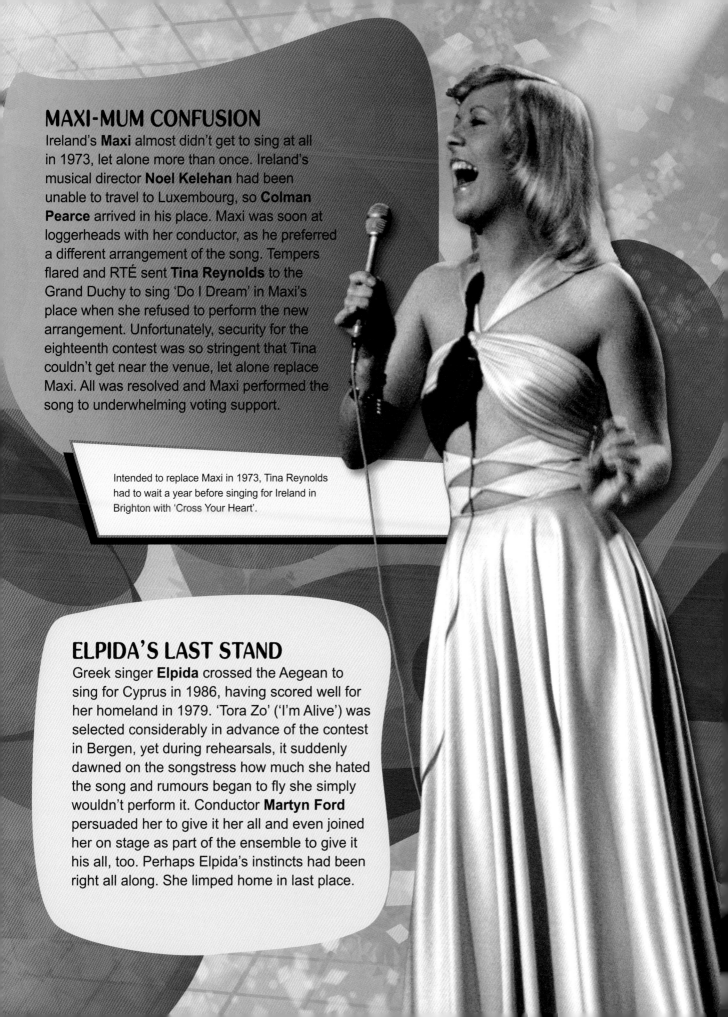

MAXI-MUM CONFUSION

Ireland's **Maxi** almost didn't get to sing at all in 1973, let alone more than once. Ireland's musical director **Noel Kelehan** had been unable to travel to Luxembourg, so **Colman Pearce** arrived in his place. Maxi was soon at loggerheads with her conductor, as he preferred a different arrangement of the song. Tempers flared and RTÉ sent **Tina Reynolds** to the Grand Duchy to sing 'Do I Dream' in Maxi's place when she refused to perform the new arrangement. Unfortunately, security for the eighteenth contest was so stringent that Tina couldn't get near the venue, let alone replace Maxi. All was resolved and Maxi performed the song to underwhelming voting support.

Intended to replace Maxi in 1973, Tina Reynolds had to wait a year before singing for Ireland in Brighton with 'Cross Your Heart'.

ELPIDA'S LAST STAND

Greek singer **Elpida** crossed the Aegean to sing for Cyprus in 1986, having scored well for her homeland in 1979. 'Tora Zo' ('I'm Alive') was selected considerably in advance of the contest in Bergen, yet during rehearsals, it suddenly dawned on the songstress how much she hated the song and rumours began to fly she simply wouldn't perform it. Conductor **Martyn Ford** persuaded her to give it her all and even joined her on stage as part of the ensemble to give it his all, too. Perhaps Elpida's instincts had been right all along. She limped home in last place.

All Out Of Luck

DISQUALIFIED ENTRIES AND ENTRANTS

Sometimes you need more than a good song and a charismatic act; to win you must also have a healthy portion of good luck.

Nicole & Hugo celebrate their last place finish from 1973 at Eurovision's 50th anniversary gala 'Congratulations' in 2005.

MARCEL, MANUEL AND I

Marcel Amont and **Joan Manuel Serrat** might be Eurovision's most unfortunate singers. Marcel was chosen to represent France in 1960 and Joan Manuel got the same invite from Spain in 1968. They were both dropped in favour of **Jacqueline Boyer** and **Massiel** respectively – singers who went on to triumph in the contest. I wonder what Marcel and Joan Manuel are doing now.

NO NICOLE

Nicole & Hugo missed out on their chance to sing for Belgium in 1971 when Nicole was stricken with jaundice just days before rehearsals began in Dublin. **Jacques Raymond & Lily Castel** stepped in, with Lily not even having time to buy a new frock. They placed 14th of the 18 entries, which was considerably better than **Nicole & Hugo**'s last place when they finally got to sing in 1973 with 'Baby, Baby'.

REPLACED PERFORMERS:

France 1960	Marcel Amont
Sweden 1961	Siw Malmkvist
Spain 1968	Joan Manuel Serrat
Belgium 1971	Nicole & Hugo
Iceland 1994	Sigrun Eva Armandsdottir

Tamar Vadachkoria, the original lead singer of Georgian band Eldrine, was replaced by Sophio Toroshelidze after being selected for the 2011 contest.

MAKING YOUR MIND UP

Recently, Belarus have made a habit of changing their minds after their national selections. In 2005, 2010, 2011, 2012 and 2013 the winning songs apparently chosen to go forth and conquer were all substituted for alternative options. When their song 'Cheesecake' was selected in 2014, most fans ignored the result, assuming **Teo**'s entry wouldn't be going to Copenhagen. Even he was probably surprised when it did.

THE BEST DUETT CAN GET

When **Duett** performed their song 'Das Beste' ('The Best') in the 1990 Austrian final, drama ensued when one of the ensemble collapsed on stage. After a break, she returned not only to perform the song again, but to win the ticket to Zagreb. Alas, hours later, the song was disqualified. If this decision caused another fainting fit, it wasn't publicly noted.

THE DISQUALIFIED, WITHDRAWN & REPLACED ENTRIES

Spain 1963	'Nubes De Colores'	Jose Guardiola
Italy 1967	'Non Pensare A Me'	Claudio Villa
Norway 1968	'Jag Har Aldri Vært Så Glad I No'En Som Deg'	Odd Børre
France 1974	'La Vie A Vingt-Cinq Ans'	Dani
Germany 1976	'Der Star'	Tony Marshall
Turkey 1979	'Seviyorum'	Maria Rita Epik
Greece 1982	'Sarantapente Kopelles'	Themis Adamantidis
Belgium 1985	'It Was Een Kind'	Mireille Kapellen
Greece 1986	'Wagonlit'	Polina
Cyprus 1988	'Thimame'	Yiannis Dimitriou
Austria 1990	'Das Beste'	Duett
Switzerland 1992	'Soleil, Soleil'	Géraldine Olivier
Greece 1997	'An Den Agapissis, Den Tha Agapissi'	Dimosthenis Stringlis
Hungary 1998	'Csak Neked!'	Erika Zoltan
Germany 1999	'Hor Den Kinden Einfach Zu'	Corinna May
Bosnia-Herzegovina 1999	'Starac I More'	Hari Mata Hari
Lithuania 2002	'We All'	B'Avarija
France 2004	'Laissez-Moi Le Temps'	Jonatan Cerrada
France 2006	'Nous C'Est Vous'	Virginie Pouchain
Serbia & Montenegro 2006	'Moja Ljubav'	No Name

Malta withdrew from the 1973 contest and Tunisia withdrew in 1977, both without having selected their entries.

WITHDRAWN FROM THE SEMI-FINALS

Belarus 2005	'Boys And Girls'	Angelica Agurbash
Lebanon 2005	'Quand Tout S'Enfuit'	Aline Lahoud
Georgia 2009	'We Don't Wanna Put In'	Stefane Da 3G
Hungary 2009	'If You Wanna Party'	Márk Zentai
Hungary 2009	'Magányos Csónak'	Kátya Tompos
Belarus 2010	'Far Away'	3+2
Ukraine 2010	'I Love You'	Vasyl Lazarovich
Ukraine 2010	'To Be Free'	Alyosha
Belarus 2011	'Born In Bielorussia'	Anastasiya Vinnikova
Belarus 2012	'All My Life'	Alyona Lanskaya
Belarus 2013	'Rhythm Of Love'	Alyona Lanskaya
Bulgaria 2013	'Kismet'	Elitsa & Stoyan
FYR Macedonia 2013	'Imperija'	Esma & Lozano

Armenia withdrew from the 2012 semi-finals without having selected their entry, as did Bosnia-Herzegovina in 2014.

IT'S THE TAKING PART THAT COUNTS

No Name scored handsomely for Serbia & Montenegro in 2005, placing 7th with 'Zauvijek Moja' ('Forever Mine') on behalf of the Montenegrin viewers. When they won the combined national heat again the following year with 'Moja Ljubavi' ('My Love'), thanks to some dubious scoring of the Serbian offerings by the Montenegrin jurors, a riot ensued and the boy band fled the stage under a siege of missiles. The decison was taken to withdraw from the contest. In sympathy, the European Broadcasting Union (EBU) allowed the country to cast their televotes anyway, thus becoming the only country ever to vote without taking part.

When Montenegrin boy band No Name won the 2006 Serbia-Montenegro heat, the Serbian audience turned ugly and the lads fled to safety.

Cry Baby

BAD LOSERS

It must be hard losing Eurovision. All those months of rehearsals, press interviews, TV appearances, radio spots and then the pressure of representing your country. No wonder so many entrants have turned pretty bitter when the ball rolled in the opposite direction on the night.

Blue's Lee, Duncan, Antony and Simon all smiles ahead of their performance in 2011.

Lena Valaitis just needed 5 more points to win.

THEY BLUE IT!

Boy band **Blue** reformed specifically to represent the UK in 2011, hoping to recreate the glory years that had seen them top the UK charts repeatedly in the earlier part of the 21st century. Probably no British act ever worked or tried so hard on behalf of an expectant nation. By the time they stepped on to the Düsseldorf stage for the jury final on Friday night to sing 'I Can', they were clearly exhausted and indeed they couldn't. Rather than accept defeat gracefully, the boys in blue took the "furious option" and decried the political voting as bitter accusations flew. Perhaps they were too tired to notice that Bulgaria had given them their sole 12 points; hardly a normal British or Western European ally.

FEELING BLUE

Lena Valaitis was tipped by almost everyone to score Germany's first victory in Dublin 1981. But perhaps because of singing third or foolishly keeping all her clothes on for her performance of 'Johnny Blue', she lost out by 4 points to skirt-ripping **Bucks Fizz**, thanks mainly to the scores from her Swiss neighbours. Lena took the loss well, but the German delegation did not. A crew from the BBC had been dispatched to Dublin to help RTÉ out with the production logistics and reported back their astonishment at the German team's anger. Fair enough, though; if you'd been Europe's most powerful nation and were waiting 26 years for a Eurovision win, you might be pretty fed up losing to a strip of Velcro, too.

CRY BABIES

Perhaps most justifiably of all Eurovision losers, Britain's **Jemini** took their defeat most to heart. "Nul points" for the UK (arguably Europe's biggest pop music nation) seemed unthinkable and yet **Chris Cromby** and **Gemma Abbey** failed to earn a single point in the largest yet field with 'Cry Baby'. The reaction from the British media was vicious and the hapless duo did their best to defend their off-key and indeed off-kilter performance in Riga 2003. Even their anger that their dressing room had been trashed during the show by a jealous rival turned embarrassing, when a member of their own troupe owned up. Alas, their humiliation was complete and indeed continuous.

MORE THAN A DREAM

Amaury Vassili was the young tenor representing France in 2011, one of the rare recent French entrants installed as a pre-contest favourite. Everyone was willing to overlook that his song 'Sognu' ('Dream') bore more than a passing melodic similarity to **Ravel's** *Bolero*, but when the juries overlooked his song and he placed 15th, he was in no mood to be gracious. "Disappointment made me vomit" was one of his less graphic comments. What he said about the winners **Ell/Nikki** and his own jury can't be printed here. His next plan was to record a duet with his partner in the hall of shame from the class of 2011, Spain's **Lucía Pérez**. We're still waiting.

DOLAN IN THE MONEY

Ryan Dolan may have been down when he placed last in Malmö 2013, but for once, he had something to cheer about and didn't opt for the bitterness route. The night before his humiliation, he was enjoying a night out in Sweden with his brother Sacha, who suddenly received a call from home to tell him he'd won almost £80,000 on the National Lottery. "It was a nice consolation prize," admits Ryan. "Performing in Eurovision was all about getting my name out there and it's done the trick." There were no losers in the Dolan family, something one or two others may like to reflect on.

Ryan Dolan sang last and finished last in Malmö, with 'Only Love Survives'.

That Sounds Good To Me

THE PERILS OF SINGING LIVE

Unfortunately for many a Eurovision act, the one thing that has remained completely constant in 60 years of competition is that no matter what else, all vocals **must** be performed live. Fair enough for a song contest, but it's amazing how many entrants that has caused one or two headaches for over the years.

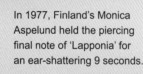

In 1977, Finland's Monica Aspelund held the piercing final note of 'Lapponia' for an ear-shattering 9 seconds.

LEAVE US BREATHLESS

Sophie Carle had the always tricky job of defending Luxembourg's title on home ground in 1984 and just to make things harder, she was drawn in the cursed second spot of the draw. Maybe that's why she veered off key singing '100% d'Amour' ('100% Of Love') to such an extent that it's really remarkable that her breathy, tuneless voice scored her 10th place in the field of 19.

LOST KEYS

Winning Eurovision doesn't necessarily require completely on-key vocals – perhaps reiterating that it is the song which wins the contest, not the singer. However, the lads from **Milk & Honey** did little to enhance the lead vocal of **Gali Atari** in 1979 when 'Hallelujah' scored a back-to-back win for Israel. **Re'uven Gvitrz, Shmulik Bilu** and **Yehuda Tamir** seemed to each be singing in a completely different key to each other, let alone Gali, but their flat tones clearly didn't bother the juries untowardly.

Bucks Fizz show off their medal for winning the UK's heat *A Song For Europe*.

VELCRO-A-GO-GO

Bucks Fizz have never denied that how they sounded on stage in Dublin 1981 was not something that gave them great pride. **Cheryl Baker** cheerfully admits that she sang her vocal in a considerably different octave to her bandmates. Thankfully for 'Making Your Mind Up', the group had nailed their presentation masterfully and with their energetic jive routine and deploying two pieces of Velcro, eked out a 4-point victory for the UK's fourth contest win.

THE LAST RASP

Yugoslavia sent **Ida & Vlado** to sing 'Ciao, Amore' ('Bye, Love') in Serbo-Croat to Luxembourg in 1984. Let's just say the pair had disparate singing styles: Ida had a soft, smokey tone, Vlado rasped in a broken voice. The duo had already raised eyebrows with a preview video that depicted them both naked and skinny-dipping. The mismatched sounds knocked them down to one place from last.

Bonnie Tyler asked Europe's judges to 'Believe In Me' in 2013. They didn't.

ON THE ROCKS

By the time **Bonnie Tyler**'s lengthy and hugely successful international career brought her to Eurovision in 2013, even her legions of global fans were admitting the 62-year-old's voice was fading. Self-describing her individual sound as being akin to "rocks and honey" (helpfully the title of her album released just before the contest), the hoarse, rasping sound of her live performance of 'Believe In Me' left the viewers and juries cold. The "hoarse" had clearly bolted on Bonnie's singing voice indeed.

Rise Like A Phoenix

WAITING TO WIN AGAIN: THE INTERMINABLE YEARS

Eurovision nations need to be patient. The roster of competing countries now stands at 51. Even leaving aside those that do not take part, this means if every country won once in turn, a Eurovision victory would come around barely twice a century.

Monster rockers Lordi finally took Finland to first place in 2006 with 'Hard Rock Hallelujah'.

GOOD LORDI

Finland first entered the contest in 1961 and was hopelessly out of synch for 45 years. Not once did they reach the Top 5 until **Lordi** changed everything with victory for 'Hard Rock Hallelujah'. Alas, Finland reverted to type the following year, earning the 7th worst result for a host nation, and they haven't placed in the Top 10 since.

MY FIRST NUMBER ONE

Greece's wait for victory stretched to 31 years until they celebrated the 50th contest in style with an emphatic win for **Helena Paparizou** and the appropriately titled 'My Number One'. It sparked a new-found appreciation for Greek songs in the contest and they remain one of the few nations with a 100% qualification record from the semi-finals, but alas, no further victories.

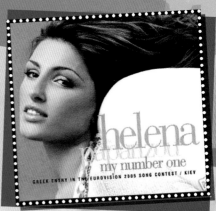

helena
my number one

GREEK ENTRY IN THE EUROVISION 2005 SONG CONTEST / KIEV

COLD TURKEY

Turkey was another country kept out in the cold, waiting from 1975 to 1986 to reach the Top 10 for the first time and then from 1986 to 1997 to do it again and rise into the Top 5. Televoting made all the difference for the Turks and finally in 2003, victory was theirs with 'Everyway That I Can' from **Sertab Erener** and her belly dancers. There were further near misses, but the Turks have since left the contest, apparently for good.

CONCHITA'S A HIT!

Switzerland and Denmark both waited well over 30 years to win twice. Just shy of a half-century after **Udo Jürgens** hit gold for Austria in 1966, **Conchita Wurst** finally scored their double, some 48 years later. In the interim years, there had been a number of Austrian withdrawals, a couple of "nul points" and nothing better than 5th place to show for their efforts. Victory in 2014 saw Conchita Wurst's nation 'Rise Like A Phoenix' to end nearly five decades of losing entries. It was even sweeter because the Austrians hadn't even qualified in 2013, joining Finland in achieving the best ever improvement from one contest to the next.

LONGEST WAIT FOR A FIRST WIN

Finland (Debut 1961 – First win 2006)	45 years
Greece (1974 – 2005)	31
Belgium (1956 – 1986)	30
Yugoslavia (1961 – 1989)	28
Turkey (1975 – 2003)	28
Germany (1956 – 1982)	26
Norway (1960 – 1985)	25
Sweden (1958 – 1974)	16
Russia (1994 – 2008)	14
Monaco (1959 – 1971)	12
United Kingdom (1957 – 1967)	10

STILL WAITING FOR THAT FIRST WINNER

Portugal (Debut 1964)	50 years
Malta (1971)	43
Morocco* (1980)	34
Cyprus (1981)	33
Iceland (1986)	28
Bosnia-Herzegovina (1993)	21
Croatia (1993)	21
Slovenia (1993)	21
Hungary~ (1994)	20
Lithuania (1994)	20
Poland (1994)	20
Romania~ (1994)	20
Slovakia~ (1994)	20
FYR Macedonia~ (1998)	16

*only competed once
~took part in the semi-finals and qualifiers before reaching the final

Austria's second winner came close to a half-century after the first. Conchita Wurst became Eurovision's first drag winner.

Why Do I Always Get It Wrong?

UNLUCKY COMPOSERS

Winning isn't everything and many, many composers have tried their hand many, many times at writing the winning song, without ever achieving their goal.

It wasn't fourth time lucky for Peter, Sue and Marc in 1981, and Switzerland's most regular Eurovision group finally got the message.

TIME TO FACE THE MUSIC

One Swiss maestro determined to triumph at all costs was **Peter Reber**. One third of the group **Peter, Sue and Marc**, Reber penned six Swiss entries from 1971 to 1981, but never rose higher than 4th place. Peter didn't just pen songs for his own group, also writing Swiss entries for other artists. Reber introduced the Alpine Horn to Eurovision in 1977 with his song 'Swiss Lady' performed in German by **The Pepe Leinhard Band**, a male sextet in six different hats. In 1980, he teamed up with **Véronique Müller**, who herself had sung for Switzerland in 1972, to compose 'Cinema' for **Paola del Medico** in Den Haag. Another 4th place was achieved. His second 4th placed entry, sung with Sue and Marc in 1981, signalled the end of his Eurovision road.

ZERO FOR HERO

Frederik Kempe is one of many Swedes who just can't resist Eurovision, but unlike a lot of his countryman, he simply can't persuade the judges to love his songs. Even having a former winner on board didn't help. When **Charlotte Nilsson Perrelli** returned to Eurovision in 2008, Kempe's 'Hero' proved unheroic for everyone and she placed 18th. It got worse in Moscow, 2009, when his co-writer **Malena Ernman** dropped back to 21st with the operatic 'La Voix' ('The Voice') sung in English. He switched to Norway for their home entry in 2010, 'My Heart Is Yours', but 20th in Oslo was pretty embarrassing, and he was welcomed back to Sweden for his two most recent entries, both of which finished 3rd. **Eric Saade's** 2011 song 'Popular' was just that and **Sanne Nielsen's** 'Undo' was a vote-catcher too in 2014. The message is clear: unless you're a hero, stick to one-word titles, Frederik.

Former Eurovision winner Lulu hosted the UK heat in 1975, where the Shadows reunited to sing 'Let Me Be The One'.

CURTIS AND CO.

Paul Curtis is the UK's most prolific Eurovision writer, but his regular pronouncements that "This one will do it" have never translated into the success he (or his country) hoped for. All looked good when **The Shadows** performed his first ever Eurosong in 1975, 'Let Me Be The One'. They placed 2nd in Stockholm, but when Paul returned in tandem with **Graham Sacher** in 1984, his song 'Love Games' was booed from the stage by a very hostile Luxembourg audience. In both 1990 and 1991, Paul's efforts went forth for a grateful British nation, only to find he'd missed the mark. He tried an environmental "green theme" in 1990, while the rest of the field was singing about freedom and unity and 'Give A Little Love Back To The World' got an environmentally unfriendly 6th. He then plumped for starving children and world hunger in 1991 to place 10th; perhaps the lyric of 'A Message To Your Heart' was just too off-putting. Certainly actress **Samantha Janus'** singing was off-key and maybe that sparkling pink corset simply wasn't the right costume for the theme. Paul remains the UK's biggest Eurovision wannabe, having written 22 entries in the UK national finals over his career. Some people just can't take a hint.

NO WAY JOSÉ!

Charlotte Nilsson won for Sweden in 1999, but came back as Mrs. Perrelli in 2008 to place 18th.

Portugal's Eurovision record is pretty atrocious. Not one of their 40 finalists has ever risen higher than 6th place. **José Calvário** can take a lot of the credit for that failure, as he's penned seven of their entries over the years. He failed right from the outset, with his 1969 ditty 'Desfolhada Portuguesa' ('Portuguese Nature') finishing 15th in a field of 16. 1971 was better when 'Menina' edged into the Top 10, placing 9th in Dublin. He did pretty well with his third effort 'A Festa Da Vida' ('The Joy Of Living') in 1972, placing 7th in Edinburgh for **Carlos Mendes**, the highest rung Portugal had yet climbed. In 1974, his song 'E Depois Do Adeus' ('After The Goodbye') started a revolution at home (really! It was used as a signal for a coup d'état to begin), but placed last in Brighton. He tried once more in 1977, but his ode to the revolution he'd inadvertently started three years earlier, 'Portugal No Coração' ('Portugal In My Heart'), couldn't manage higher than 14th. His last entry proved worst of all. 'Voltarei' ('I'll Return') finished 18th in 1988. José never returned.

It's Just A Game

ENTRANTS WHO TAKE IT SERIOUSLY

When host Harald Treutiger introduced the 1992 contest in Malmö, he welcomed everyone to "the greatest game show in the world". Eurovision is a lot of fun and hugely entertaining for the viewers, but some of the entrants have taken it all rather too seriously and personally.

Jahn Teigen & Anita Skorgan set aside their own horrendous Eurovision track records to earn 12th place in 1982.

FRENCH KISS AND MAKE UP

Britain's **Nicki French** seemed very eager to place the blame anywhere she could when she achieved what was (at the time anyway) the UK's worst showing: 16th place in 2000 with 'Don't Play That Song Again'. It was because the UK didn't support the Euro, she claimed. It may have slipped her notice, but none of the top four placed countries that year were Euro adopters either. The winner's Denmark remain firmly in the Eurosceptic club with the UK even now. Still, Nikki remains a huge Eurovision enthusiast and turns out for the fans at every opportunity, even if the result left her crushed at the time.

BITTER SWEDE SYMPHONY

Jahn Teigen perhaps had most reason to feel bitterness towards the contest, but in fact, turned his humiliation into a resounding success. Although by no means the first singer ever to fail to score, he did so under the far more generous "douze points" system, ending up with a big zero in 1978. He admitted at the time that when he realized what was likely to happen, he panicked because Sweden was the last to vote that night. Had they come to a neighbourly rescue, his achievement would have been ruined. They didn't. Even neighbours sometimes draw a line. Fame and fortune (or rather infamy and misfortune) followed, but Jahn ruined it all by coming back to Eurovision twice more, eventually placing 9th in 1983. Regardless, he's a lot better remembered than most of the class of 1978.

LONG MEMORIES

Another bitter Brit is **Sir Bruce Forsyth**, whose daughter Julie wrote the UK entry 'Go' in 1988 for **Scott Fitzgerald**. The one-point loss was crushing, and Scott vented his anger for readers of Britain's tabloid newspapers in the ensuing months. For Sir Bruce, the rancour was longer-lasting. Appearing on the BBC's *Room 101* decades later, he asked to consign Yugoslavia to Orwell's chamber of horrors in retaliation for their scoring. Eurovision wounds run deep.

FIGHTING FOR IRELAND

Boxer **Barry McGuigan** was a wee lad when his Dad **Pat McGeegan** arrived in London to sing 'Chance Of A Lifetime' for Ireland in 1968. Barry can thus be forgiven for being a little cloudy on the details of what actually happened at the Royal Albert Hall that fateful April night. Barry's recollection of his father leading in the voting is certainly random, as is his assertion that Pat finished in 3rd place. It's true that Ireland were at a high of 2nd at one brief moment during the voting, but 4th was where they ended up. Might be wise not to break it to Barry. He can be quite useful with his fists.

HERE COMES THE BRIBE

t.A.T.u's manager and producer **Ivan Shapovalov** was certainly a master of media manipulation. Having got his act to the top of the world's charts via whirlwinds of media activity surrounding their lesbian lifestyle, he brought them to Eurovision 2003 in Riga. Rehearsals were fraught – when the girls even bothered to attend – and his PR machine ground its way through the week, keeping his charges on the front pages of every European newspaper. When the expected victory didn't come, many who were there in the Skonto Olympic Hall claim to have witnessed Shapovalov's fury explode. Blame was apparently laid at the feet of Russian TV who, it is claimed, he berated backstage for not having paid a big enough bribe to the organizers. Quite how a bribe to the EBU could possibly influence the televoters at home wasn't made clear and there's no real evidence that his outburst ever happened; perhaps his bitterness at losing was more to do with the end of the international road for his two decidedly heterosexual artists.

t.A.T.u. assumed victory would be theirs in 2003, but the girls placed 3rd, just 3 points separating them from the trophy – the closest ever contest.

Lohengrin Filipello hosted the very first contest in 1956 alone. In 2014, three hosts were needed in Copenhagen: Johan Philip 'Pilou' Asbœk, Lise Ronne and Nikolaj Koppel.

— CHAPTER THREE —

Hosting & Voting

From famous rivalries between nations to mind-blowing interval acts, troublesome televoting to songs sung in strange made-up languages, Eurovision shows that when it comes to the nations of Europe competing for glory, they'll try anything.

That's What Friends Are For

NEIGHBOURLINESS AND RIVALRIES

Ask anyone on the street what they think of Eurovision's scoring and they'll probably tell you "it's all political". Whether this is the case is open to debate, but there is always the belief that a great song can win over anybody.

FRIENDS OR FOES

Ireland have always been fairly half-hearted about their British neighbours and you won't find too many top marks heading to their former, unwanted overlords. Not so in the other direction. Seven times the UK have declared "douze points" for their Irish chums. Ironically, as Ireland struggled in the 1976 contest, the British awarded them their second highest score of the night. In return, as the UK stormed to the biggest ever win under the current voting system, Ireland felt they simply couldn't offer any more than 3 points in return. They saved their 12 for Italy, who coincidentally, were the only other nation not to put 'Save Your Kisses For Me' in their Top 4. Strange that. It was best not to ask the late **Lynsey de Paul** if she recalled the UK giving Ireland 12 in 1977 only for her song 'Rock Bottom' to get zero in return.

Lynsey de Paul teamed up with Mike Moran to sing for the UK on home ground in 1977.

LOVE THY NEIGHBOUR

In 1966 this neighbourly voting was particularly evident for the first time when Denmark, Norway, Sweden and Finland clubbed together and Northern and Southern Europe pretty much divided along geographical lines. For once, even Ireland felt neighbourly enough to give their top score to the UK. Something they've only done once since.

TOO CLOSE TO CALL

The German-speaking nations of Germany, Austria, Luxembourg and Switzerland have generally practised more of a "loathe thy neighbour" approach to the contest. Televoting may have shifted that stance, but for decades, the four nations could generally be relied upon to snub each other musically. Indeed, when **Nicole** crushed all opposition in 1982, she did so with a single point from Austria (much to the hilarity of the Harrogate audience) and nothing at all from next door Luxembourg. The only other mark less than 8 came from another neighbour, 6 points from the Netherlands. Fair enough, really; after all, Austria won without a single point from Germany in 1966.

FINANCIAL DAILY

ROCK BOTTOM

TWELVE POINTS

Turkey and Azerbaijan have become best Eurovision friends since the Azeris joined the contest in 2008. In every final (and semi-final) in which they've both appeared, they've generously exchanged 12 points faithfully. Sadly for Azerbaijan, Turkey's withdrawal from the contest after Baku 2012 has left them without their most reliable score. They certainly won't find it from Armenia. Their mutual loathing hasn't yet generated a single point in any direction.

LET'S STICK TOGETHER

Certainly it's true that the Scandinavian and Baltic nations do their fair share of vote back-slapping every year, but perhaps not always as much as one might believe. In 1963, the Nordic bloc made up a quarter of the field and thus controlled 25% of the votes, so maybe it's no surprise Denmark won. But how would anyone explain that Sweden, Norway and Finland all ended the night without a single point between them? Or indeed that Norway and Finland still top the charts for the most number of last places and "nul points"?

IRATE IRA LOSCO

Malta had high hopes of a victory in 2002 and sat just three points behind Latvia on 171 when the final nation of the night, Latvia's neighbours Lithuania, was called upon to decide the contest. If **Ira Losco** had thought she could still pull it off, she might have known instantly she heard the words "This is Vilnius calling" that she was going home empty-handed. Lithuania snubbed her song and awarded Latvia's **Marie N** 12 points for the gold.

The Maltese were very cross indeed when lacy Ira Losco narrowly lost out on victory in 2002.

If I Could Choose

THE TELEVOTERS vs THE JURIES

Since televoting was trialled in 1997, the contest has largely been determined by the viewers at home watching. It was very clear even from the 1997 experiment with five televoting nations, that already there was a diversion from the juries and viewers.

THE VOTES ARE IN...

Everybody seemed to agree in 1997 that the UK had the winning song, but others appealed to either the televoters or the juries, not both. Iceland picked up 18 points, 14 from two of the five televoting nations and 4 from just 2 of the 20 juries. Ten of Denmark's 25 points came from 3 of the televoters. The die was cast.

THE JURY'S OUT

From 1998 to 2008, pretty much every country televoted. The only exceptions were the rare instance of lack of phone coverage or a technical error. Back-up juries existed in every country, just in case; and it was apparent that although everyone was agreeing with who'd won (generally) the rest of the field was not so clear cut. In 2009, the juries were given 50/50 equal shares in the voting with the televoters, with 5 "music industry experts" comprising each national jury.

Norway's Alexander Rybak achieved a score of 387 points, a tally that has yet to be bettered.

BIG SCORE

The 50/50 voting split worked well in Moscow, 2009. Since Norway's 'Fairytale' from **Alexander Rybak** crushed all opposition in a manner never seen before, nobody could take issue with any of the scoring. Particularly as some of the Big Five nations (or some of the four that took part: Germany, UK, Spain and France) improved their fortunes after some truly dreadful results at the hands of the televoters alone. **Lord Andrew Lloyd-Webber** took the UK back into the Top 5 and **Patricia Kaas** also crept into the Top 10 for France.

France's Twin Twin tried tall quiffs in 2014, but placed last with 'Moustache'.

THE QUIFF TWINS

Identical twins **Jedward** appeared in successive contests, in 2011 and 2012, and the televoters warmed to their quirky quiffs both times. The voters placed them 10th in Düsseldorf and 10th again in Baku. The experts felt very differently. Their debut 'Lipstick' earned them 7th with the juries, and their follow-up 'Waterline' was greeted with disdain and 25th place.

GREASY TURKEY

As had long become the norm, Greece and Turkey's diaspora was enormously useful in the televoting in 2012. They shot up to 9th and 4th respectively with those watching from their homes and online, whereas the experts with no allegiance to any motherland but their own, placed the rivals 18th and 20th. Turkey withdrew from the contest and hasn't been seen since, despite the combined scoring giving **Can Bonomo**'s 'Love Me Back' 7th place.

PICK 'N' MIX

New transparency made things much easier in 2014. In addition, the top picks of the juries and viewers were more or less in synch. Austria's 'Rise Like A Phoenix' rose to the top of both lists, lighting the flame for **Conchita Wurst's** international breakthrough. The Dutch got 2nd overall, 2nd with the viewers and 3rd with the experts. Since Sweden's **Sanne Nielsen** was 4th at home and 2nd in the jury room, naturally she was 3rd in the total tally with 'Undo'. Likewise, Armenia's **Aram MP3** placed 3rd in the televote, 5th with the juries and finished 4th in the contest with 'Not Alone'. Nobody at all was alone in mistaking any of what had happened; it was all very clear.

Dilara Kazimova failed to 'Start A Fire' and became Azerbaijan's first entrant not to place in the Top 8.

HOME FIRES BURN BRIGHT

In 2014 it was only Malta and Azerbaijan who could rightly feel confused. The Maltese were very unpopular with the televoters, placing 24th, but the experts thought very highly of 'Coming Home' and placed **Fire Light** 6th. Somehow, it all panned out to 23rd in the final shake-up. Similarly, Azerbaijan's **Dilara Kazimova** managed to 'Start A Fire' with the juries to attain 8th, but her ardour was dampened by the viewers who placed her 22nd, which is where she ended overall.

Are You Sure?

THE RESULTS ARE IN

It's probably no wonder that the morning after every Eurovision Song Contest, millions of viewers across Europe and beyond are scratching their heads in bemusement over the result. After all, things got off to a very questionable start.

NOT-QUITE-CONGRATULATIONS

The only question in the run-up to the 1968 contest seemed to be, Who would finish second to the UK's **Cliff Richard**? The German jury had other ideas and with Cliff leading for most of the second half of the scoring, Germany awarded 6 of their total 10 points to Spain's **Massiel**, giving her a one-point margin. Despite confusion over Yugoslavia's scores next, Spain triumphed with 'La, La, La…' over Britain's 'Congratulations'. Years later, a Spanish documentary team claimed German TV had been bribed with programme purchases to vote for Spain's song. It would have explained a great deal had it been true. Ironically, when the UK press was looking for a scapegoat, it was Ireland's jury who took the blame, even though they'd magnanimously awarded 1 point to each of the top two songs. Can't say fairer than that. It was the basest ingratitude by the Germans, who received 5 of their total of 11 points from the UK.

HANDY SCANDIES

Having overseen the last contest with Mr. Stockselius at the helm, 2010 Executive Supervisor **Jon Ola Sand** replaced him in 2011 as the contest's supervisor and scrutineer, the third Scandinavian to hold the post.

SWISS BLISS

In 1956, the judges came to the host venue and watched the show from the audience, rather than on TV. There were two judges representing each of the seven participating nations, but apparently, Luxembourg didn't send anybody to deliberate on their behalf, so the Swiss judges covered for them. The Swiss winning on home ground with 'Refrains' by **Lys Assia** was surely a coincidence?

The UK's Cliff Richard lost by 1 point in 1968, yet consoled himself when 'Congratulations' went on to sell a million.

KING ROLF

Every time the contest scoring veers towards calamity, it's the EBU's scrutineer to whom everyone turns. **Rolf Liebermann** was the Jury President for the inaugural and second contests in 1956 and 1957 and presumably it was he who verified that Luxembourg's Swiss judges had fairly attributed their scores.

NUL POINTS FOR MARCHAL-ORTIZ

Christine Marchal-Ortiz became the first woman to oversee the contest, scrutinizing from 1996 to 2002. Her first contest was not her finest moment, when it transpired after the show that Spain's 6 points were in fact meant for 'Holland' and not Poland as hostess **Ingvild Bryn** had supposed. Still, since Mrs. Marchal-Ortiz' new broom had seen Germany and Russia – Eurovision's largest viewing nations – knocked out in an audio-only qualifier, that was the least of her worries.

A FOUR-WAY TIE

Winning by one point in 1968, Spain couldn't separate themselves from the field at all on home ground in 1969 and had to share their second victory with France, the Netherlands and the UK. A four-way tie in a field of only 16 songs was unimaginable and hostess **Laurita Valenzuela** was so incredulous, scrutineer **Clifford Brown** had to reassure her of the result three times. The result led to a mass walk out of nations in 1970.

In 1969, Maria Rosa Marco Poquet became Salomé and got a quarter share of the four-way tie for 1st place, Spain's last winner to date.

EUROVISION SCRUTINEERS

1956–1957	Rolf Liebermann (Jury President)
1958–1962	Unknown
1963–1965	Miroslav Vilcek
1966–1977	Clifford Brown
1978–1992	Frank Naef
1993–1995	Christian Clausen
1996	Christine Marchal-Ortiz
1997	Marie-Claire Vionnet
1998–2002	Christine Marchal-Ortiz
2003	Sarah Yuen
2004–2010	Svante Stockselius
2011–2015	Jon Ola Sand

The Party's Over Now

EUROVISION HOSTS WITH THE MOST

From reluctant repeat hosts to €60 million state-of-the art facilities built especially for the competition, Eurovision hosts have approached the task in very different ways...

HOST WITH THE MOST

The BBC's **John Peel** was dispatched to produce a documentary of the 1987 contest in Bruxelles. Two years later, when doing the same in Lausanne, he came across a familiar face in the Belgian team. French-speaking Belgium had won the contest in 1986, but it was the Flemish half of the country whose turn to select their entry had fallen the following year. A battle ensued for which broadcaster would host and where, with the French station RTBF winning out, but Dutch language channel VRT selecting the home entry. Brussels played host at the Palais du Centenaire exhibition complex and were left with a huge financial headache. According to Peel's confidant, bills were still not paid two years on, and RTBF were still reeling financially from staging the contest. Seems they weren't alone.

MONEY, MONEY, MONEY

Ireland won three Eurovisions back to back from 1992 to 1994 and by the third time the host role fell into their lap – despite much speculation that they'd actually chosen a song that could never, ever hope to win in 1994 – RTÉ were in serious financial trouble. The Irish National Lottery helped out, but the government had to step in with a tax increase to help fund the rest. A fourth victory in 1996 left the coffers pretty empty and Ireland have studiously managed to avoid picking up the Eurovision bill ever since.

ELEPHANT IN THE ROOM

Money seemed to be no object at all for Azerbaijan's AiTV in 2012, producing the most expensive Eurovision Song Contest ever. Perhaps the real cost of the contest will never be known, but estimates of 60 million Euros being spent on the complete production are typically quoted. The entire city was given a spectacular makeover, but the jewel of the reconstruction was a brand new 20,000-seat arena, built from scratch in less than twelve months. The rather closed nature of Azeri society didn't allow too much foreign media inspection of what was really being paid out, but the estimates can only be a fraction of what was actually spent. The Baki Kristal Zali is generally regarded as a very expensive, unwanted white elephant.

Baku underwent a costly facelift to prepare for Eurovision 2012, including building from scratch a 20,000-seat indoor arena The Baki Kristal Zali.

BELGRADE NEEDS AN UPGRADE

Rumours were rife that Belgrade would miss their chance to host the 2008 contest, when civil unrest erupted in the city months before the contest was due to take place. Right-wing activists targeting immigrants were at the root of the trouble, hardly a welcoming gesture for Europe's favourite TV show. Peace was quickly restored to Belgrade's streets, long before rehearsals got under way, but the right wing, anti-gay campaigners, backed by a hostile local press, made their voices clearly heard during Eurovision week. Belgrade failed in their bid to show only a positive side of their city to the world.

Eimear Quinn triumphed with 'The Voice', Ireland's seventh victory – and their last to date.

CROATIA COSTS CASH

Financial woes had hit Zagreb's Eurovision plans long before a single note was sung at the 1990 competition. Now Croatia's capital, the city was playing host because Yugoslavia had won the previous year with Croatian band Riva. During rehearsals, hosts **Helga Vlahović** and **Oliver Mlakar** publicly resigned after discovering a younger pair of presenters were being secretly rehearsed behind their backs, causing much international amusement and embarrassment for JRT. Costs spiralled and bills couldn't be paid even before the show got under way. A last-minute cash injection from the region's tourist board saved the day, but their spokesperson admitted they didn't understand why they hadn't been asked to contribute earlier. Hours after the show ended, the executive producer **Goran Radman** was fired from JRT's affiliate RTZ over the financial debacle.

GAME OVER

When Düsseldorf was chosen as the host city for the 2011 contest by ARD/NDR, they too had to build a new stadium from scratch. Not to host the Eurovision Song Contest, but to house the local football team they were displacing by taking over the Esprit Arena for more than a month. A vast, but temporary stadium was erected around a practice soccer pitch in the shadow of the arena so that the football season continued uninterrupted by the songs of Europe.

Somewhere In Europe

EUROVISION'S SHIFTING BORDERS

Despite most viewers still scratching their heads as to how this determinedly geographically Asian nation could even be taking part in Eurovision, Israel has a hat trick of wins.

TINY DANCERS

The tiny nation of Israel scored the first of three wins just five years after their debut, catching many by surprise in Paris, 1978, as rank outsiders for the 23rd title. **Izhar Cohen & Alpha Beta** proved all the tipsters wrong by charging to victory with 'A-Ba-Ni-Bi', much to the disgust of Jordanian television, who had taken a commercial break whilst the all-singing, all-dancing troupe had strut their stuff during the competition. When the victory was apparent, Jordan pulled the plug on the broadcast, continuing their evening viewing with a photograph of a bunch of daffodils. Perhaps equally astonishing, Israel retained the title in Jerusalem, 1979, at the first contest staged outside Europe's borders.

MOROCCAN SPICE

Two wins in a row is rare in Eurovision, yet having done it, Israel withdrew from the contest in 1980. They'd already passed the mantle on to the Netherlands' broadcaster NOS, citing financial constraints, but when the Dutch hosts chose April 19th for the 25th anniversary show, Israel had to bow out because it clashed with one of their holiest days of the year. With Israel out of the field, Morocco stepped in. 'Bitakat Hob' (Love Card) was the one and only Arabic song ever performed at Eurovision. The North African Kingdom appeared on the contest stage, but when singer **Samira Bensaid** limped home with just 7 points from an impressed (yet bizarrely wayward) Italian jury, Morocco pulled up their tents and have yet to return.

SO-BE-IT UNION

Unlikely as it seems, the former Soviet Union made several attempts to take part in Eurovision in the 1980s, despite publicly decrying the contest as it gained popularity in the 1960s and doing their best to block the TV signals from the EBU. The idea was seriously proposed in 1987, but not until the end of the Union did any former Soviet nation enter the contest in 1994.

FLYING TURKEY

A small part of Turkey falls into Europe, but the biggest part of the nation is distinctly Asian territory. Their 1975 debut at the contest was largely ridiculed with just 3 points and when they returned in 1978, they earned 1 point less. From the 1980s they began to move away from the bottom rung, but it wasn't until televoting was introduced in 1997 that Turkey's vast European diaspora came to their rescue. **Sertab Erener** squeaked a narrow win of 2 points in 2003, with 'Everyway That I Can' bringing the show to Istanbul the following year. When the 50/50 jury split saw them fail in the 2012 semi-final, Turkey withdrew from the contest and, by all accounts, aren't keen on coming back.

LUCKY PAIR

Aysel & Arash were the oddly physically mis-matched duo chosen separately to perform Azerbaijan's 2nd Eurovision entry 'Always' in 2009 and flung together abruptly for the final in Moscow. The quickly manufactured chemistry paid dividends and the pair found themselves in 3rd place, albeit way adrift of the record point-scoring Norwegian winner. Azeri TV realized they were on to something and paired another disparate duo together **Ell/Nikki** two years later to sing 'Running Scared' and claim their first win.

AySel showing more than just a bit of leg while partnering Arash to Azerbaijan's first Top 3 finish in Moscow 2009.

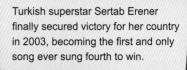

Turkish superstar Sertab Erener finally secured victory for her country in 2003, becoming the first and only song ever sung fourth to win.

On Again... Off Again

SHOWSTOPPERS

Cost headaches seem to have been a problem for Eurovision right from the beginning. However, it's not always the money that's the problem for the host broadcaster.

France's Josiane Grizeau morphed into Monaco's only winner Séverine in 1971.

PASS THE DUTCHY

In 1970, Dutch TV eagerly drew the right to stage the 15th Eurovision Song Contest and started plans for Amsterdam. However, the debacle over the four-way tie that had seen a quarter of the entries go home winners in 1969 was not over. Austria, Finland, Norway, Portugal and Sweden all refused to enter the 1970 competition, joining the already departed Denmark on the sidelines. Swedish broadcaster SR claimed the contest was dying on its feet. Dutch hosts NOS agreed that they would produce the show on the proviso that it was not a funeral for the contest. It wasn't. NOS injected spectacular new production values into the proceedings and Eurovision found a hugely popular winning song in Ireland's 'All Kinds Of Everything'. The contest was back on track and all the boycotting nations returned in 1971, with Malta joining their ranks.

OUT IN THE OPEN

In 1972, tiny Monegasque broadcaster TMC bravely tried to put together a production in the face of lack of technical resources and know-how. With the support of the Principality's Royal Family, the palace was offered as the first venue, along with Monte-Carlo's Opera House and a temporary open air arena in the palace grounds. The EBU rejected the outdoor plans, but regardless, TMC looked hopefully to their French neighbours for technical, financial and logistical support. By most accounts, French TV were more than willing to help, but only if they took on the full mantle of the host and the contest was moved into France and full acknowledgement given for having provided every component of the 1971 victory. Stalemate was reached, so in stepped the BBC, offering to host in the Scottish capital of Edinburgh, with full credit to Monaco's winner: **Séverine**'s winning entry opened the show and she presented the Grand Prix at the end. Unfortunately, during the show, her interest was clearly waning when cameras caught her checking her watch when Monaco's entry was performed.

WE'RE ON OUR WAY TO WEMBLEY

In 1977, the BBC was hosting the contest for the sixth time, on this occasion in the North London suburb of Wembley. A brand-new conference centre had recently opened in the shadow of the world-famous football stadium and excitement was building as the UK's own selection contest took place in March. Alas, seconds before that show was due to go live, a lightning strike was called by cameramen. The industrial action spread throughout the BBC and the proposed broadcast date of April 2nd for the 22nd contest was shelved. Dutch TV stepped in with an offer to play host instead, but their unions immediately stood firm with their British allies. The 1977 contest was officially abandoned. Thankfully, just days after the cancellation announcement, all was resolved and a new contest date of May 7th was quickly arranged. It was the latest the show had taken place since 1956, but in subsequent years, May became the standard month for the competition.

In 2002, Jessica Garlick scored the UK's only Top 3 finish in the new millennium.

British industrial action almost prevented Marie Myriam scoring France's record-breaking fifth victory in 1977.

GOVERNMENT HANDOUT

When Estonia became the first former Soviet satellite to win the contest in 2001, many observers doubted the tiny nation could possibly stage the contest. Prime Minister **Mart Laar** took personal charge of the operation and guaranteed his government would underwrite the entire cost of staging the 2002 show in his capital, Tallinn. Thankfully, a local brewery took on naming rights of the brand new Suurhall, the venue for the 47th contest, injecting some much needed cash, but even co-host **Marko Matvere** admitted to the BBC that his fee was being covered by the government. The year's entire tourism budget was allocated to the production and with a huge influx of tourists to the city in subsequent months, all Estonians seemed to agree it was money very well spent.

Come Back To Stay

UNUSUAL HOST CITIES AND VENUES

Who wouldn't turn up the chance of several hundred million viewers in multiple countries to promote themselves? It's the main reason why broadcasters embraced the contest so eagerly and cities vie for the chance to host.

LIFE IN TECHNICOLOUR

Colour broadcasting in 1968 brought the interval act into full PR mode, with the BBC commissioning *Impressions From London,* a film to show off the capital in full colour for the first time to international TV viewers. Alas, colour sets were still an expensive rarity amongst the estimated 200 million viewers, and in the UK itself BBC1 was incapable of carrying a colour signal at the time, so even British viewers had to wait for the next day's repeat on the colour channel BBC2 to see the show in its intended colourful glory.

LUGANO SAY YES

It wasn't long before the host broadcaster also saw the potential audience as a chance for promoting the host city. Lugano, the small Swiss city in the Italian-speaking canton, put itself on the map by hosting the very first contest in 1956, albeit with little ability to show anything except the interior of the Teatro Kursaal to the watching millions.

MILLSTREET ON THE MAP

Tiny Millstreet is possibly the most unusual host city, being little more than a village way to the west of Ireland's capital Dublin. The owner of the Green Glens Arena was determined to bring the contest to his town and the whole community came together to help overcome all the logistical challenges, which included rebuilding the railway station so that the domestic Irish audience could attend en masse. The impact of the tiny town on the world's audience was huge and largely overshadowed the contest itself, attracting many new visitors to Ireland's west.

PICTURE POSTCARDS

Riga is one of Europe's oldest capitals, yet not particularly familiar to the mass audience tuned into the 2003 contest. Latvia's LTV plans to show the world all it and Latvia had to offer were scuppered late in the day, when the postcards prepared for the contest were rejected by the EBU. In their place, the competing singers were filmed in and around Riga during the week of rehearsals, a far more lacklustre ad for Latvia's delights. The original postcards were shown online on the official website as compensation.

WOMBLES GO TO HARROGATE

Whereas two of Britain's capitals, London and Edinburgh, and the second city of Birmingham have all hosted the contest, the smaller towns of Brighton and Harrogate also got their chance to shine for the international audience. The Harrogate contest of 1982 appropriately opened with the question "Where is Harrogate?", heralding a very lengthy explanation that showed off all the tourist delights of Yorkshire. Brighton's history and royal palace provided a charming backdrop for the 1974 show, but seeing the interval act **The Wombles** prancing around the beaches and town may have potentially put any visitors off from booking their holidays.

OFF-MESSAGE PT. 1

Without doubt, the most nationalistic contest ever staged was the show in Baku 2012. Azeri TV, bankrolled by a generous and wealthy government, took every opportunity to show the world what this little nation on the Caspian Sea had to offer, and the inter-song postcards highlighted all the nation's delights. Human rights activists, though, were determined to have their voices heard, somewhat detracting from the official image the Azeris wanted to promote.

OFF-MESSAGE PT. 2

The second time they hosted the contest, the Swiss chose the small city of Lausanne on the shores of Lake Geneva. The longest ever filmed introduction for the show included Swiss cheese, Heidi and other stereotypes, but the inclusion of a visit to the local chocolate manufacturer Toblerone was cut by orders of the EBU just before transmission. Unfortunately, nobody thought to tell the commentators the segment wasn't airing, leaving many floundering live on air.

Cliff Richard and Belgium's Claude Lombard outside London's Royal Albert Hall, 1968.

Parlez-Vous Français?

THE LANGUAGES OF EUROVISION

Twenty-four languages are officially recognized by the European Union. Several Eurovision entries have eschewed the mainstream languages and indeed have gone as far as making up their own entirely.

A FULL ENGLISH

The influx of new countries to the contest, beginning in 1993, brought new languages and cultures to the competition. In 1994, Lithuania placed last. Its second entry, in 1999, was sung in Samogitian and placed 20th. Not surprisingly, the country has chosen to sing in English ever since.

LOST IN TRANSLATION

Having been banned from Spanish entries by **General Franco**, Catalan finally made it to the entry list in 2004 with Andorra's song 'Jugarem A Estimar-Nos' ('We'll Be Playing At Love') by **Marta Roure**. She failed to qualify for the final, as indeed did all her fellow Andorran wannabes, even those who later switched to singing in English. Andorra soon got the message and left the competition.

DIALECTS DIE OUT

Local dialects also play their part in Eurovision music. Austria's 1971 entry 'Musik' ('Music') was performed in Viennese and in 1996 they tried Vorarlbergish for 'Weil's Dr Guat Got' ('When You're Doing Well'), with Italy's 'Comme È Ddoce 'O Mare' (How Sweet Is The Sea) being sung in Neapolitan in Rome 1991. France tried Haitian Creole French in 1992 with 'Monté La Rivie' ('Cross The River') and Corsican for 'Mama Corsica' in 1993, but otherwise have stuck to French or, lately, English.

SINGING IN TONGUES

With so many languages to choose from, it seems surprising that Eurovision writers haven't been shy in coming up with one entirely of their own. Three entries to date have been sung in completely imaginary tongues, with the first providing strong encouragement for those that followed. 'Sanomi' from **Urban Trad** became Belgian's second most successful Eurovision entry when they were pipped at the post in 2003. Neck and neck with Russia and Turkey throughout the scoring, Belgium lost out by 2 points to **Sertab Erener**'s Turkish winner on the final vote, the closest contest since its 1993 expansion.

SÉVERINE TIES

Monaco won Eurovision singing in French in 1971 and never varied from their majority language, despite Italian being an official option for their songs. When they briefly returned to the contest's semi-finals in the new millennium, they switched from French to Tahitian for **Séverine Ferrer**'s 2006 entry 'La Coco-Dance' ('The Coco Dance'). Alas for this **Séverine**, she was unable to recreate her namesake's victory from 35 years earlier and after losing in their third straight qualifier, Monaco haven't bothered to enter at all since.

AWKWARD!

Since the rule requiring entries to be sung in their national language was abolished in 1999, the unfortunate occurrences of lyrics in their native tongue sounding distinctly awkward to foreign ears has largely abated. Maybe it explains why Iceland's 'Hægt Of Hljótt' ('Slowly And Quietly') scored badly in 1987. **Halla Margrét Árnadóttir** was actually singing the line "einu sinni, einu sinni enn" and not indeed something sounding far more anatomically uncomfortable to English ears.

The 1971 Eurovision Song Contest winner, Severine, with previous winner Dana.

Happy Man

EUROVISION COMPOSERS AND THEIR SONGS

Some composers seem very happy to have cornered the market in Eurovision music. Their successes (and failures) just couldn't stop them coming back for more.

I WRITE THE SONGS

Dutchman **Willy van Hemert** was the first composer to secure two victories in Eurovision, writing the victorious Dutch songs 'Net Als Toen' ('Just Like Then') and 'Een Beetje' ('A Little') in 1957 and 1959, albeit with two different partners, **Guus Janssen** and **Dick Schallies**. Together, van Hemert and Schallies also penned the Netherlands' 1960 entry 'Wat Een Geluk' ('What A Lucky Thing') but placed 12th of the 13 entries in London. Schallies returned in 1961 with **Piet Goemans** to pen 'Wat Een Dag' ('What A Day'), this time placing 10th out of 16 entries. Willy's son Hans followed in his father's footsteps, writing Dutch Eurovision songs 'I See A Star' and 'The Party Is Over Now'.

Ralph Siegel & Bernd Meinunger have jointly penned 15 finalists, including 2nd place for Germany's Lena Valaitis.

RUN AND HIDE

Siegel's lyricist is more often than not **Bernd Meinunger,** aka **John O'Flynn**. He paired with Siegel for their first Eurovision contest in 1979 and the bloodthirsty 'Dschingis Khan' ('Genghis Khan') by the similarly named group. He penned 15 more entries with Siegel, but his 17th and last song for the contest was written with **David Brandes**. 'Run & Hide' was sung by Gracia in 2005, but the song placed last in the contest and earned all sorts of criticism and penalties when it emerged Brandes had attempted to manipulate the track's chart success.

SIEGEL-VISION

The Daddy (or maybe now the Grand Daddy) of Eurovision music is Germany's **Ralph Siegel**: 22 of his compositions have been selected for Eurovision from six different nations, 19 of them making the grand final. He also submitted songs to a plethora of other nations that he failed to impress. Despite his persistence, Siegel has just one win to his credit, the hugely successful 'Ein Bißchen Frieden' ('A Little Peace') for Germany's **Nicole** in 1982. It was the fourth consecutive year he'd won the German national final, with his two previous entries being very narrowly pipped at the post. His German entry 'Lass Die Sonne In Dein Herz' ('Let The Sun Shine In Your Heart') also placed 2nd in 1987. Reputedly, German TV refused any more of his efforts after 2004, so in recent years his name has appeared on the credits for Switzerland, Montenegro and San Marino.

SWINGS BOTH WAYS

Rolf Løvland won with his first Eurovision finalist 'La Det Swinge' ('Let It Swing') in 1985, ending years of Norwegian misery. Despite failing to win again in 1987 and 1994 (and conducting the orchestra for songs he didn't pen in 1992 and 1993), he got his second win with **Peter Skavlan** in 1995 and 'Nocturne'. Løvland can easily challenge **Johnny Logan**'s claim to be the only performer to win Eurovision twice, as he appeared on stage for both his victories, albeit playing the keyboards rather than singing.

LOGAN'S RUN

Johnny Logan (aka **Sean Sherrard**) wrote two winners of course (and sang a third), but he's not alone in this achievement for Ireland. **Brendan Graham** also penned two winners, 1994's 'Rock & Roll Kids' and 1996's 'The Voice'. His two earlier efforts 'When?' in 1976 and 'Wait Until The Weekend Comes' in 1985 both hit the Eurovision Top 10 but were pretty far away from the winning podium.

FIRST AND LAST

Maurice Vidalin and **Jacques Datin** penned Luxembourg's first Eurovision winner in 1961 and attempted to defend their honour the following year in the Grand Duchy. They managed 3rd place but sensibly accepted they were beaten and were never seen in Eurovision again.

Australian-born Irishman Johnny Logan has won three times and penned a runner-up.

WINNING AUTHORS/COMPOSERS CONDUCTING THEIR OWN SONG

KLAUS MUNRO	'Après Toi'	LUXEMBOURG 1972
NURIT HIRSH	'A-Ba-Ni-Bi'	ISRAEL 1978
KOBI OSHRAT	'Hallelujah'	ISRAEL 1979
ATILLA SEREFTUG	'Ne Partez Pas Sans Moi'	SWITZERLAND 1988

SINGING DOLL

Possibly Eurovision's most famous victorious songwriter, **Serge Gainsbourg** penned 1965's winning entry for his muse and goddaughter **France Gall**. 'Poupée De Cire, Poupée De Son' ('Wax Doll, Singing Doll') was a hit several years before the steamy 'Je T'Aime Moi Non Plus' was banned by the BBC. He could also lay claim to have invented 'Boom Boom, Bang Bang' for Eurovision with 5th-placed Monegasque song 'Boum-Badaboum' in 1967. 23 years later he returned in Zagreb with 'White And Black Blues' for France's **Joelle Ursull** and had to settle for joint 2nd place but the biggest hit of the class of 1990. Pretty good compensation.

Serge Gainsbourg with France Gall, who led from start to finish in 1965 and brought swinging 60s pop to Eurovision.

ONE IN SEVEN

Britt Lindeborg, Stefan Berg, Geir Lengstrand and **Peter Boström** all scored victories for Sweden in partnership with other writers and all of them wrote other Swedish entries to no avail. **Thomas G:Son**, however, not only wrote 'Euphoria' for **Loreen**'s huge win in 2012 (with Boström) but penned many other songs for many other countries. Norway, Spain, Denmark and Georgia have all accepted his efforts, bringing his total to seven entries for four countries, but crucially, just one win.

CÉLINE POUR MOI

Nella Martinetti and **Atilla Sereftug** petitioned to have their 2nd placed song 'Pas Pour Moi' ('Not For Me') installed as the winner when it was revealed they'd been beaten by a 13-year-old and not a 15-year-old singer as first thought. The petition was dismissed, so they entered a French Canadian in 1988 with 'Ne Partez Pas Sans Moi' ('Don't Leave Without Me') and bit their nails to the quick as **Céline Dion** won by one single point on the very last vote. They got their win and thus retired from Swiss Eurovision duty.

LOREEN
EUPHORIA

CANDLE IN THE WIND

Yoav Ginai and **Svika Pick** were the musical brains behind **Dana International**'s iconic 1998 victory with 'Diva', but when they came back in 2002 with **Sarit Hadad**'s 'Light A Candle' their winning team was snuffed out. Pick turned his attention to Ukraine's 2003 debut song 'Hasta La Vista' and slipped back further to 14th.

WRITTEN OR COMPOSED MOST WINNERS		
WILLY VAN HEMERT	2	THE NETHERLANDS 57, 59
YVES DESSCA	2	MONACO 71, LUXEMBOURG 72
JOHNNY LOGAN (aka SEAN SHERRARD)	2	IRELAND 87, 92
ROLF LØVLAND	2	NORWAY 85, 95
BRENDAN GRAHAM	2	IRELAND 94, 96

WINNING AUTHORS/COMPOSERS PERFORMING THEIR OWN SONG		
UDO JÜRGENS	'Merci Chérie"	AUSTRIA 1966
LENNY KUHR	'De Troubadour'	THE NETHERLANDS 1969
BENNY ANDERSSON & BJÖRN ULVAEUS (ABBA)	'Waterloo'	SWEDEN 1974
MARTIN LEE & LEE SHERIDAN (Brotherhood of Man)	'Save Your Kisses For Me'	UNITED KINGDOM 1976
JOHNNY LOGAN	'Hold Me Now'	IRELAND 1987
TOTO CUTUGNO	'Insieme 1992'	ITALY 1990
ROLF LØVLAND^ (Secret Garden)	'Nocturne'	NORWAY 1995
KIMBERLY REW* (Katrina & The Waves)	'Love Shine A Light'	UNITED KINGDOM 1997
JØRGEN OLSEN (The Olsen Brothers)	'Fly On The Wings Of Love'	DENMARK 2000
MARIJA NAUMOVA (Marie N)	'I Wanna'	LATVIA 2002
SERTAB ERENER	'Everyway That I Can'	TURKEY 2003
RUSLANA	'Wild Dances'	UKRAINE 2004
MR. LORDI (Lordi)	'Hard Rock Hallelujah'	FINLAND 2006
DIMA BILAN	'Believe'	RUSSIA 2008
ALEXANDER RYBAK	'Fairytale'	NORWAY 2009

*ALTHOUGH A REGULAR MEMBER OF KATRINA & THE WAVES, KIMBERLY REW DID NOT ACTUALLY APPEAR ON STAGE WITH THE BAND IN THE CONTEST, BUT HIS GUITAR PLAYING WAS FEATURED ON THE BACKING TRACK USED IN DUBLIN.
^ROLF LØVLAND WAS ALSO ON STAGE FOR HIS 1985 WINNER 'LA DET SWINGE' BUT RECEIVED NO CREDIT FOR THIS PERFORMANCE ACCOMPANYING BOBBYSOCKS.

WINNER OF THE
EUROVISION SONG CONTEST
2001

everybody

TANEL PADAR & DAVE BENTON

EVERYBODY'S A WINNER

Maian Anna Kärmas and **Ivar Must** teamed up just once to deliver Estonia's one and only victory to date in 2001 with 'Everybody' for the ill-matched **Dave Benton & Tanel Padar with 2XL**. They wrote other Estonian entries without success, but never together.

Making Your Mind Up

SHOWSTOPPING INTERVAL PERFORMANCES AND ACTS

Few remember Les Joyeux Rossignols et Les Trois Menestrels. There's really no reason to. Their footnote in the contest's history book is achieved by being the first ever interval act. In 1956, they entertained the viewers while while the 14 judges made their minds up.

STUCK IN THE MIDDLE

The idea of an interval act didn't catch on quickly. Until 1961, the only other interval entertainment came in 1958, halfway through the performances of the 10 entries and again after they'd all appeared, when the **Metropole Orchestra** under the direction of **Dolf van der Linden** performed a couple of short interludes, including 'Ceilito Lindo' ('Lovely, Sweet One').

DANCE WITH THE STARS

Ireland typically roots back into their Celtic heritage for their interval acts, with a visit to Shannon Castle being the highlight of the 1971 break. The balletic *Timedance* from **Planxty** in 1981 highlighted Ireland's dance history for the first time, but modern music also plays a part in Irish productions. **The Hot House Flowers** performed 'Don't Go' in 1988, in a video filmed across the Eurovision nations and beyond; whereas host **Ronan Keating** joined his **Boyzone** mates to sing 'Let The Message Run Free' in 1997, bringing some contemporary elements to Ireland's host productions.

Irish boyband Boyzone was the interval act in 1997, when member Ronan Keating played host.

SINGIN' IN THE RAIN

In Copenhagen 2014, **Emmelie De Forest** invited all the participating singers and performers to join her on stage for 'Rainmaker' live on the set of the converted shipyard, the B&W Hallerna. The water surrounding the set certainly played a big part in the spectacle that brought all the hopeful nations together as they prepared to learn their fate.

STRICTLY COME DANCING

Riverdance tops almost every poll as the interval act everyone can remember. **Bill Whelan**'s musical extravaganza was led by the Celtic choir **Anuna** and Irish dancers **Michael Flatley** and **Jean Butler**. It is almost impossible to describe the scene unfolding on the stage when performed live in 1994, but when it reached its crescendo the audience leapt to their feet and gave a deafening reception the likes of which had never been heard before in Eurovision. Backstage, Executive Producer **Moya Doherty** was completely flabbergasted by the audience reaction, but admitted she realized at that point she was on to a good thing!

Eurovision's most successful interval act, Riverdance made Michael Flatley a star.

DANCING DOWN UNDER

In recent years, the winning artist from the year before is more often than not the key part of the interval, although with the introduction of the semi-finals and longer and longer voting windows, there are now multiple intervals in each show. In 2014, Australia joined in the contest when **Jessica Mauboy** performed 'A Sea Of Flags' on behalf of the huge audience down under, after viewers saw the Aussies moving their land right to the heart of Europe.

A CLASS ACT

Classical acts often prove a relief from the pop music of the contest and opera star **Mario del Monaco** not only filled in while the scores were being tallied in 1965, but also presented the Grand Prix to the winners at the climax of the show. **The Vienna Boys Choir** performed chorale music at the 1967 contest, whereas jazz provided the inspiration for **Les Haricots Rouge (The Red Beans)** in 1965, **Acker Bilk & His Paramount Jazz Band** in 1977 and the luminaries **Stephane Grapelli, Yehudi Menuhin** and **Oscar Peterson** in 1978.

Mister Music Man

MUSICAL CONDUCTORS

The appearance of the conductors was an integral part of the contest from its inception in 1956, but with the way TV and even music was being made in the new millennium, it was time for the Chef d'Orchestre to move on.

NUMBER ONE CONDUCTOR

Dolf van der Linden became synonymous with Eurovision, conducting for the first 20 years of the contest. He holds the record for having conducted for the most number of countries, seven in total, spanning 19 songs. He was also the first ever conductor to score two victories and made it three when he took on the responsibility for Ireland's first win in 1970. More famous perhaps for his role as the leader of **The Metropole Orchestra**, van der Linden revived the interval act in 1958 and composed the incidental music for that and the 1970 contest in Amsterdam. He retired from the podium the following year.

STRIKE UP THE MUSIC, MAESTRO!

Noel Kelehan was Eurovision's greatest ever conductor, waving the baton 29 times for five different nations and for five different winners, also acting as the contest's overall musical director on a record four occasions. Noel was the maestro for Ireland most years from 1966 to 1998, and when the contest was staged in Ireland he often had to step in if a nation had not sent its own conductor or – as in the case of Bosnia-Herzegovina in 1993 – had left their musical director on the tarmac as the team escaped under gunfire.

TO BE FRANCK

France's **Franck Pourcel** was another highly regarded and notable musician who became closely associated with the early years of the contest. He was there from the very start, conducting the first French entries in 1956 and quickly conducting his way to a then record three wins by 1962. Franck made 1972 his last Eurovision outing, but not before leading the musicians 23 times for 6 different countries. In addition, he scored several hit singles with instrumental versions of various entries, including several winners.

Franck Pourcel conducted 23 different Eurovision entries for 6 different nations, including 4 winning songs for France.

Sven-Olof Walldoff met his Waterloo in 1974, conducting for Sweden's first winner dressed as Napoleon.

WALLDOFF'S WATERLOO

In 1974, **Sven-Olof Walldoff** saw his opportunity to grab the spotlight when asked to conduct the orchestra for Sweden. It was also a very, very smart way to lodge the Swedish entry in the judges' minds. Not that they needed much help, as the performing group themselves were pretty much doing enough already, but every little helps. Before **ABBA** made their entrance to sing 'Waterloo', Sven-Olof walked to the podium dressed as **Napoleon**, to the delight of audience. Since ABBA's victory was a slim 6 points over Italy, it may possibly have been the gimmick that gave them the edge.

BULLET PROOF

Only minutes after the first, Eurovision's second lady conductress struck up the orchestra when **Nurit Hirsh** directed Israel's debut song 'Ey Sham' ('Somewhere') from **Ilanit**. Hirsh had penned the music herself, but didn't appear to be wearing a bullet proof vest, as it was suggested was the case for the singer. Nurit composed the music and conducted again five years later, becoming Eurovision's only lady to conduct a winning song as 'A-Ba-Ni-Bi' stormed home to victory. Since then, only **Anita Kerr** has tried her hand as a female musical director, for Switzerland in 1985.

Israel's Ilanit earned 4th place in 1973, under the baton of the only woman to conduct a winner, Nurit Hirsh (in 1978).

All Ireland's shame was personified in 2008 by the failure of Dustin the Turkey to reach the final. The puppet singer's plans to have his giblet removed and come back as Dustin International came to nothing.

## CHAPTER FOUR

Weird & Wonderful

If you love weird dancing, shock fashion styles,
over-the-top artists going crazy and songs
about boomerangs, look no further
– Eurovision has it covered.

Wild Dances

CRAZY ONSTAGE CHOREOGRAPHY

Choreographic excess is almost synonymous with Eurovision music. The two seem to go hand in hand. Here are some of contest's most famous – and infamous – movers.

A DANCE IN THE RIGHT DIRECTION

In 1966 both Denmark and the Netherlands tried a few smart moves. **Milly Scott** became the first ever black entrant in the contest and bounced around the set of the Ville du Louvigny in Luxembourg with the contest's first hand microphone. Such was Milly's dexterity that at the end of the song, she bounced backwards up the stage stairs, all the while still singing. Denmark's **Ulla Pia** had gone further and brought two dancers with her, the first ever performers on the Eurovision stage who didn't sing or play an instrument. Again, it didn't catch on immediately, but the impact was made.

HIGH FIVE

The higher definition that arrived with colour broadcasting in 1968 brought a new found freedom of movement to the contest, aptly demonstrated in the 1970 interval act by **The Don Lurio Dancers**, who created what is possibly Eurovision's most frenetic dance display in its long history. When the rules were relaxed to allow five performers on stage in 1971 – no matter what their rôle – the floodgates didn't open, but they were widening. The **Koivisto Sisters** provided some great moves for Finland, albeit as the backing singers for **Markku Aru**.

THE FIRST DANCE

In the contest's early days, only soloists or duets were permitted to perform for each country, with no more than three backing singers or musicians. Not much room allowed for too many dance steps, but it didn't stop Germany's **Alice & Ellen Kessler** trying out some nifty moves in 1959, the first choreography of the competition. Placing 8th out of 11 songs was hardly impressive, but it wasn't long before others were following the German sister's approach.

Germany's Alice & Ellen Kessler danced their way to 8th place with 'Heute Abend Wollen Wir Tanzen Geh'n' (Tonight We Want To Go Dancing) in 1959.

IT STARTED WITH A KISS

Brotherhood of Man became not only the contest's biggest-winning hit makers with their winning song 'Save Your Kisses For Me', but also kick-started a whole new approach for performing contestants. The group readily admit that they were astonished when first shown the steps they were expected to follow by their choreographer in the UK heat, but they overcame their reluctance and ran away with the trophy there and later in Den Haag, launching a hugely successful and lengthy international career. They later mused that their routine was the forerunner of *Riverdance*.

RAISING THE BAR

When Germany's **Dschingis Khan Gruppe (Ghengis Khan)** arrived in Jerusalem, the group had already caused some offence at their mere selection. The Israelis were perhaps justified to be angry at the thought of a German song about a bloodthirsty, murdering ruler and yet the show created by the sextet brought the house down. Taking choreography to a whole new level, the group pretty much staged a three-minute Broadway Musical and the bar was raised for all who would follow. Again however, popular though **Dschingis Khan** was to earn 4th place, it was the far simpler steps of **Gali Atari** with **Milk & Honey** that won out.

LAST TANGO IN HARROGATE

Spain's **Lucia** brought a tango demonstration to Harrogate 1982, whilst Israel's **Avi Toledano** was the all-singing, all-dancing, all-smiling Israeli artist who took choreography up another notch, performing a pop version of the traditional Israeli 'Hora'. At the last contest to utilize microphones with cables, the BBC audio crew did their best to capture the singer's vocals, but such was the exuberance of Avi's dancers that the strategically placed stand mics were sent flying into the audience by some wayward high kicks. Regardless, Avi finished in 2nd place.

The all-singing, all-dancing Israeli entries of the 1980s began with Avi Toledano's 'Hora' in Harrogate, 1982.

A DANCE TO REMEMBER

Carlos Paião and his four backing singers hadn't really got the hang of Eurovision dancing in Dublin 1981, but they gave huge entertainment value nonetheless. Sticking their microphones in their ears with staccato hopping and jumping on the spot was never going to be a winner for 'Playback', but thankfully video editors everywhere had a clip ready for eternity whenever a demonstration of what not to do in the contest was needed.

LOOK AT THE STARRS

Tommy Seebach & Debbie Cameron joined forces for Denmark, bringing dancers to Dublin 1981 – dancers who threw themselves around the set with such liberated abandon that by the time they had finished their breathless routine, it's likely nobody could remember the actual song. **Emly Starr** did the same for Belgium, with her two exotic dancers at least registering visually with their dresses slit to the hips. Even though both nations fared badly, the die was cast and more and more dancers began appearing.

PUTTING YOUR FEET UP

The UK got into choreography in a big way in 1980 when **Prima Donna** went to Den Haag with 'Love Enough For Two' and dance moves enough for six. Completely unrated by the British public ahead of the final, the moves the three boys and three girls put together certainly impressed and they astonished everyone – possibly even themselves – with 3rd place, setting a trend for dancing Brits that dominated the decade.

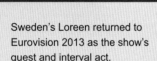

Sweden's Loreen returned to Eurovision 2013 as the show's guest and interval act.

WESTEND WHIRLWIND

Austria's **Westend** really rolled out the dance moves in 1983 for 'Hurricane' with the five lads in their bright yellow outfits joined by dancer Patricia, who certainly twirled around the stage in a whirlwind. They fared better than the Turkish tribute to 'Opera' that scored "nul points" so the following year Turkey sent **Beş Yil Önce On Yil Sonra** (Five Years Before And Ten Years After) to try their hand at some smart dance moves. It took the Turks to their best result yet in 12th place with 'Halay' ('Dance').

GOOD VIBRATIONS

More and more dancers joined the contest, with **Kikki Danielsson's** backing troupers clearly emulating **Michael Jackson** for 'Bra Vibrationer' ('Good Vibrations') for Sweden in Gothenburg 1985. Although placing 3rd, the dancers left such an impression that a year later, they crossed borders to join **Lisse Haavik** for Denmark in Bergen. Alas, despite their enthusiastic help, Lisse's 'Du Er Fuld Af Løgn' ('You Are Full Of Lies') placed only 6th.

WILD DANCES

In the new millennium, it's largely been the Eastern European nations that have honed and perfected the Eurovision dance moves. **Sertab Erener's** belly dance for 'Everyway That I Can' gave her Turkey's only win in 2003, and in 2004, **Ruslana's** 'Wild Dances' set a new benchmark for dance excess as she and her fur and leather clad dancers stomped around the stage to glory. How she managed to belt out the lyric with all the frenzied activity was astonishing, perhaps one reason why the televoters were so very impressed.

Ruslana scored Ukraine's first win with only their second entry and set new standards for choreography.

ALL THE WORLD'S A STAGE

The trio of lads accompanying **Alexander Rybak**'s 'Fairytale' in 2010 took things lying down. Quite literally, providing horizontal dance steps. Yet their moves still blew the audience away. Ultimately, perhaps **Loreen**'s choreography and staging set the new benchmark for Eurovision performances in 2012. Appearing with one dancer on set, she dazzled with the visuals for 'Euphoria'. It may never get as good as that again. Although let's be honest, we know it probably will.

You Got Style

THE FASHION CRIMINALS

Singing well is all well and good, but when you have only three minutes to make an impact it is important to have a look that (you hope) will capture votes across Europe…

THE HORN BLOWS

Guildo Horn came to Eurovision seemingly with the whole of Germany behind him. Despite singing 'Guildo Hat Euch Lieb!' ('Guildo Loves You!'), the rest of Europe were unconvinced by the garish figure cut by the balding crooner on stage in Birmingham. Backed by **The Orthopedic Stockings** (his "support", geddit?) he ran around the set in impossibly stacked platform boots, a turquoise velvet cape slung around his shoulder. Underneath was a matching suit, complete with bright yellow ruffled shirt. It was all too much and whereas the promised televotes from his legions of fans who intended to cross into Germany's neighbours to boost his support failed to materialize, the Dex award was never in any doubt.

Before climbing the stage gantry, Guildo Horn came into the audience to ruffle the hair of Katie boyle, guest of honour in 1998.

STARS IN OUR EYES

Barbara Dex sang for Belgium in 1993. This shy young lady revealed during interviews that her bigger ambition was to be a fashion designer. Alas, her revelation caused barely muted sniggers when she arrived on stage in a self-designed pea green creation that defies belief, let alone description. Clearly the judges were equally stunned and her song (composed by her father) limped home last, with just 3 points. Rather than allowing the unfortunate girl to slip away quietly, the Eurovision community now annually presents the Barbara Dex Award to the most tragically dressed artist in the competition.

Michalis Rakintzis and mates performing 'S.A.G.A.P.O.'.

ROBOT WARS

Most commentators warned their audiences that when Greece took to the stage in 2002, it was **Michalis Rakintzis** singing 'S.A.G.A.P.O.' and not an attack of the clones. The bizarre leather and metal outfits for Michalis and his band were certainly more suited to a low budget sci-fi movie than the Eurovision stage. Placing 17th was better than most expected, but it was the only time Greece missed the Top 10 in the ten years from 2001. The robotic choreography was retired and Michalis presumably slipped into something a little more comfortable.

BOOBS ON SHOW

Long before the Dex award was even thought of, Spain's **Patricia Kraus** drew gasps when she appeared on stage in Bruxelles 1987, wearing a leather "boob tube" apparently made entirely from large buckled belts. 'No Estás Solo' ('It's Just Me') was an appropriate song for her but not for the outfit. The lengthy green chiffon stoll did nothing to enhance the intimidating bondage look.

Glittering Ukrainian drag act Verka Serduchka earned 2nd place in 2007.

VICTORY FOR VERKA

Verka Serduchka was already in trouble before she (or he) arrived in Helsinki for Eurovision 2007. Parodying a nouveau riche Russian housewife, drag act Verka had been selected to represent Ukraine with 'Dancing Lasha Tumbai' and insisted the title meant 'Whipped Cream' in Mongolian. That it sounded remarkably like 'Russia Goodbye' did not go unnoticed. It was hard not to notice Verka in her silver dress and huge sunglasses, with a glittering mirrored star atop her silver skull cap. Ukraine's culture minister threatened to resign if Verka (and her accompanying mother) went to Helsinki, but didn't when she did. Verka finished 2nd, got a major international hit that outsold the winner by ten to one, and took home the Barbara Dex Award and millions of new fans.

CLOWNS IN SHORT SKIRTS

Other than Switzerland winning the inaugural contest, only Serbia had ever triumphed at their first attempt, albeit having entered under other national guises in previous years. Within two years, the bubble had burst and they didn't qualify. Qualification again evaded them in 2013, but that may have had more to do with the costumes of **Moje 3** than their song 'Ljubav Je Svuda' ('Love Is Everywhere'). Quite what the concept might have been was lost on the audience as the ridiculousness of the execution overwhelmed the three girls. Was it the devil and an angel trying to tempt a fair maiden? Possibly, but what transpired was three grotesque clowns in far too short skirts and stacked heels impossible to walk in.

Serbia's Moje 3 failed to reach the final, but won the Barbara Dex award, voted by fans.

I Love The Little Things

SMALLER COUNTRIES

The Eurovision Contest Song is for countries big and small, and these supposed "minnows" have made a impact on the competition.

Greek star Vicky Leandros sang the German composed 'Après Toi' in French for Luxembourg to take victory in Scotland, 1972.

SMALL VICTORY

Luxembourg's diminutive stature makes them one of the contest's most remarkable success stories. Five outright victories makes them the second most successful winning nation in the competitions' history, despite not having been seen in the field since 1993. Like the other tiny Eurovision nations, finding local talent to represent them was never easy, yet they must have gloated when German TV rejected **Vicky Leandros'** 'Dann Kamst Du' in 1972. The Grand Duchy quickly snapped it up. Translated to French, 'Aprés Toi' ('After You') cruised home for their third win, a decade before Germany finally got their first.

FINAL RESTING PLACE

San Marino, Europe's oldest democracy nestling in the Northern Italian hills, first took up the Eurovision challenge in 2008, limping home in last place in the first semi-final in Belgrade with just 5 points. Clearly wounded, they stayed away until 2011 when they again took an early bath. For three straight years, local Sanmarinese jazz singer **Valentina Monetta** represented her 32,000 compatriots with songs composed by German **Ralph Siegel**, until at last reaching the final for the first time in Copenhagen, 2014. The celebrations continued long after she finished 24th of the 26 on the big night.

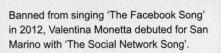

Banned from singing 'The Facebook Song' in 2012, Valentina Monetta debuted for San Marino with 'The Social Network Song'.

MALTA MATTERS

Like Austria and Portugal before them, Malta had a miserable start to Eurovision when their very first entry finished last in Dublin, 1971. Unlike any other country before or since, they followed it up with another last place in Edinburgh 1972. They never sang in Maltese again. For 1975, **Renato** performed 'Singing This Song' in English and went home a hero for reaching 12th place in the field of 19. Regardless, the Maltese skipped the next 15 years, before returning in 1991 to earn 6th place and launch a whole new approach. **Chiara** came close to winning in 1998 and went even closer in 2005 to finish 2nd, just as **Ira Losco** had done in 2003. Since then, Malta have had very mixed results, but did win the Junior Eurovision Song Contest in 2013.

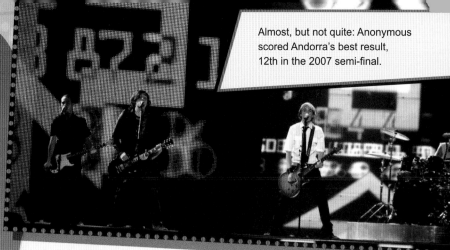

Almost, but not quite: Anonymous scored Andorra's best result, 12th in the 2007 semi-final.

ANDORRA NO MORE

Andorra, the mountainous resort nation in the Pyrenees, spent six years trying to impress the Eurovision televoters, but having been rejected at every turn, eventually gave up. Despite bringing in Dutch, British, Italian and Spanish artists, as well as introducing Catalan to the contest, voters were unmoved. The British boy band **Anonymous** took them closest to the final in 2007, placing 12th in the semi-final, two places short of their goal. Since 2009, Andorra have opted to stay away completely.

CYPRUS DOWNHILL

Unlike their Greek and Turkish neighbours, Cyprus got off to a fairly solid start in Eurovision, finishing 6th in 1981 and moving up to 5th in 1982. Since then, it's all been downhill, with only one further 5th place finish achieved in 1997. The island nation has steadfastly been supported by Greece whenever they've reached the final, but support further afield has been hard to find and with strained finances, Cyprus withdrew after the 2013 edition.

THE LEGEND OF LIECHTENSTEIN

If you're looking for tiny Liechtenstein in the Eurovision record books, you won't find them, despite some legendary rumours to the contrary. Until the 21st century, the microstate didn't even have a TV station, although since acquiring one of their own, rumours of a potential entry have consistently appeared. Contest folklore has it that Liechtenstein selected **Biggi Bachman** to perform 'Little Cowboy' at the 1976 contest in Den Haag, but with no broadcaster to submit the song it's hard to see how this story came about.

Sing Little Birdie

EUROVISION SONGS INSPIRED BY ANIMALS

Feathered friends have been a recurring Eurovision theme from the outset and Birds and other winged creatures have often appeared in the contest since…

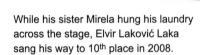

While his sister Mirela hung his laundry across the stage, Elvir Laković Laka sang his way to 10th place in 2008.

EARLY BIRD SPECIAL

'De Vogels Van Holland' ('The Birds Of Holland') was the first song ever performed at the contest, sung by **Jetty Pearl** on the stage of the Teatro Kursaal, Lugano, 1956. But, due to the mislaid results from that first competition, nobody knows how well Jetty's Dutch debut fared and if it was a subject thus truly worth pursuing.

BIRDS OF A FEATHER

Roger Pontare has twice sung for Sweden, on both occasions dressed from head to toe in feathers and furs, visually representing tribes from indigenous Americans rather than Scandinavian natives. The feathers, flames and his menagerie of similarly dressed backers, propelled him to 7th place in Stockholm 2000 with *'When Spirits Are Calling My Name'*. A marked improvement on his 12th, scored alongside **Marie Bergman** six years earlier.

BIRD SONG

'Sing Little Birdie' was the UK's second entry and the first of 15 to finish in 2nd place. **Pearl Carr & Teddy Johnson** brought along a finger puppet of their aforementioned feathered buddy, a novelty that didn't catch on but perhaps inspired the lyrics of many a future Eurovision entry. Teddy's birdsong whistling was more readily copied. Just shy of 50 years later, Ireland dispensed with the singers completely and just sent a puppet. **Dustin The Turkey** demanded 'Irlande Douze Points' ('Ireland Twelve Points') but crashed out in the semi-final with nothing higher than seven from any other country.

HIGH FLYING 'BIRDS'

Having sung about birds in their first ever Eurovision entry, the Dutch waited 58 years before trying the subject again. After eight consecutive failures to reach the final, **Anouk** not only took 'Birds' into the 2013 final but gave the Dutch their first Top 10 finish since 1999. It was clearly the right move because in 2014 the bird-named **Common Linnets** went even better and finished 2nd in Copenhagen with 'Calm After The Storm', Holland's biggest success since victory in 1975.

HUNG OUT TO DRY

The closest a real bird got to the Eurovision stage was with Bosnia-Herzegovina's 2008 entry 'Pokušaj' ('Try') from **Laka**. The EBU stepped in to bar his black hens from taking the Belgrade stage, but could do little about the accompanying pregnant brides, knitting their way to 110 points and 10th place, while **Laka's** co-conspirator hung his laundry out to dry across the set.

PARROT IN DISGUISE

Jean Paul Gaultier dressed **Dana International** in a simple black gown for her appearance for Israel in 1998 but adorned the dress with brightly coloured parrot feathers. Realizing in rehearsals that the dress was too uncomfortable, the transsexual artist opted instead for simple silver grey, agreeing to wear the parrot-themed design for the winning reprise should she win. She did, and she did.

AUSTRIA'S LITTLE PONY

Birds and insects may have merits, but steer clear of anything bigger from the natural world. Austria's debut entry in 1957 was a country and western flavoured song about a horse: 'Wohin, Kleines Pony?' ('Where To, Little Pony?') from **Bob Martin**. Not many countries have finished last on their debut, but Bob found his way promptly into Austria's stable of Eurovision shame.

TEARS OF A CLOWN

Monaco provided the first clown-related Eurovision song with 'Mon Ami Pierrot' ('My Friend Pierrot') in Cannes, 1959. Such was the juries' distaste for anything clown related, **Jacques Pils'** song finished last in the field of 11. Not to be deterred, Jacques sent his daughter **Jacqueline Boyer** to the 1960 contest and watched her triumph with a song about a real, yet lovable rascal, 'Tom Pillibi'.

Dana International delayed the 1998 finale to change into Jean Paul Gaultier's feather-adorned dress for her reprise.

Let Me Be The One

HOSTS AND PRESENTERS

The songs and the acts are the most important elements of Eurovision, but we shouldn't forget the work of its hosts and presenters, who do their best to ensure the broadcast runs smoothly.

The only person to present Eurovision 4 times, Katie Boyle hosted for Britain between 1960 and 1974.

HOSTS WITH THE MOST

To date, only two people have ever hosted Eurovision more than once. **Jacqueline Joubert** welcomed Europe to Cannes in both 1959 and 1961, whereas Italian-born **Katie Boyle** (aka Caterina Irene Elena Maria Imperiali di Francavilla, the Countess of Shannon and Lady Saunders) took on hostess duty four times from 1960 to 1974. Despite her experience, Katie's handling of the Eurovision scoring was always problematic, although perhaps less so on her last outing in 1974, when she was more concerned about having her underwear cut from under her dress seconds before her entrance.

BROKKEN COMES BACK

Several former winners of the contest have tried their hand at hosting the competition. **Corry Brokken**, 1957's winning singer was the first, coming out of musical retirement and setting aside her law studies to host the 1976 competition in Den Haag. She later announced the scores on behalf of Dutch TV NOS in 1997.

A TOTO MESS

Italy's two victors **Gigliola Cinquetti** and **Toto Cutugno** paired up to host the 1991 contest in Rome, a decision surely regretted by all involved. Neither seemed to have any grasp on the proceedings and were woefully under-rehearsed. The shambles of their presentation clearly irritated scrutineer **Frank Naef**, who was forced to repeat the scores the hapless pair repeatedly misunderstood. They really should have stuck to singing.

RIPPON TO SHREDS

Having hosted the contest on four occasions, veteran presenter **Katie Boyle** was retired by the BBC and replaced by their star newsreader Angela Rippon for the 1977 contest staged at the Wembley Conference Centre in North West London. Ms. Rippon almost missed her opportunity to host the competition when a TV strike blanked screens all over Europe. Eventually, the contest took place over a month late, in what the hostess later described as the most "under-rehearsed TV show in history." Much criticized in the British media for her poor "schoolgirl French", Angela soon after forsook reading the news and took up dancing and antiques hunting on TV instead. Eurovision will do that to you.

The BBC's Angela Rippon was flustered when winner Marie Myriam failed to appear at the climax of the 1977 contest.

Swedish hosts Anders Lundin and Kattis Ahlstrom introduced Swahili to the 2000 presentation.

CHEEKY CHAPPY

Arguably the first contest presenter to bring irony to the proceedings, **Anders Lundin** teamed with **Kattis Ahlstrom** to give a cheeky narrative to the contest presentation, which won many plaudits from fans and viewers alike. Determined not to stick to the tried and tested presenting style, Lundin showed off his language skills to the utmost, even throwing in some Swahili – "Just in case." Alas, thanks to Ahlstrom's reluctance for him to share them, his dance moves remained unseen.

MOST TIMES HOSTED THE CONTEST

BY NATION:

8	UNITED KINGDOM	1960*	1963*	1968	1972*	1974*	1977	1982	1998
7	IRELAND	1971	1981	1988	1993	1994	1995	1997	
5	SWEDEN	1975	1985	1992	2000	2013			
4	LUXEMBOURG	1962	1966	1973	1984				
4	THE NETHERLANDS	1958	1970	1976	1980				

* NATION HOSTED THE CONTEST DESPITE NOT HAVING WON THE PREVIOUS YEAR

Ding Ding-A-Dong

EUROVISION SONGS WITH BELLS ON

"Ding Dong, Eurovision calling." What is it about Eurovision lyrics and the sound of bells? Is it all the UK's fault?

FOR WHOM THE BELL TOLLS

The UK entry **Ronnie Carroll** set forth for Luxembourg in 1962 with 'Ring-A-Ding Girl', penned by the team of **Syd Cordell** and **Stan Butcher**, who's previous Eurovision lyrical masterpiece, 'Sing Little Birdie' had placed 2nd. The bells weren't ringing for Ronnie, who had to be content with joint 4th place with a song about two cigarettes glowing in the dark from Yugoslavia.

RING A DING DONG

Thérèse Steinmetz opened the 1967 contest in Vienna with what has to be the nadir of Eurovision Ring-A-Ding's, representing the Netherlands with 'Ringe-Ding'. The trite lyric contained no less than fourteen *Ring-Ding-A-Ding*s and six *Ding-A-Ding-Dong*s. Still, can't really blame **Thérèse**; the blame lays firmly with the writers **Johnny Holshuyzen** and **Gerrit den Braber**. Someone liked it. One each of the British and Irish judges picked it as their favourites. 2 points is better than none.

A WINNING DING (-A-DONG)

'Ding Dinge Dong' reappeared for the Dutch in 1975, when **Teach-In** took their lyrical masterpiece to Stockholm to open the 20th contest. Although performed in English, the song retained its Dutch title for the contest, but was translated to 'Ding-A-Dong' for the English single release. Just in case anyone was still linguistically confused, the song became 'Ding Ding-A-Dong' for the German market. Lyrically challenging or not, **Teach-In** coasted to victory, attaining the fourth (and to date last) Dutch win.

Dutch group Teach-In became the first winners to sing 1st in the running order.

Krista Siegfrids caused a
'Ding Dong' in 2013 performing
a lesbian wedding on stage.

THE BALLAD OF TOM TOM TOM

Always handicapped by their impenetrable, unique language, the Finns benefitted hugely from the relaxation of the native tongue rule in 1973, when **Marion Rung** returned for her second Eurovision with Finland's first English language entry. With the new advantage, it's baffling why 'Tom Tom Tom' was the chosen lyric for the new found contest liberation. Regardless, Marion bounced up to 6th place, setting Finland's best yet contest showing, bettered only once in the future.

After crashing out in the 2011
semi-final, Dana International
shunned all media attention.

PARADISE LOST

When the language rules were relaxed again in 1999, Finland soon scored not only their first ever victory in 2006, but their first ever place in the Top 5. So why they felt the need to revert to the trite words 'Da Da Dum' in 2011 isn't entirely clear, although **Paradise Oscar** opening the show did earn much fan praise for his gentle start to the Düsseldorf contest, even if only 21st place was attainable.

DING DONG

If ever there was a clear sign that Eurovision has finally moved on from 'Ding Dong', it came in 2011. **Dana International** (having beaten a group called **Knob** in the Israeli heat) returned to the contest 13 years on from her glorious triumph. No other winner had yet returned only to be dumped out in the semi-finals. Maybe the voters simply thought a transsexual singing 'Ding Dong' was just a joke too far. You can't make it up sometimes.

Boom Boom Boomerang

TRULY EXPLOSIVE LYRICS

There's a strange attraction in Eurovision lyrics to the explosive noun "Boom". I suppose it ensures the contest always go with a "Bang".

POP GOES THE BRITISH

Whether or not the British did invent the explosive Eurovision wording, they were the first (and to date the only) country to triumph with this clichéd and much parodied lyric. Scottish singer **Lulu** was less than impressed when British viewers chose the lyrically challenged song 'Boom Bang-A-Bang' penned by **Alan Moorhouse** and **Peter Warne** for her to perform in Madrid 1969. When she squeaked into the winner's circle to share 1st place with France, Spain and The Netherlands, she readily admitted that she was dreading the prospect of having to sing the song for the rest of her career. Thankfully for her, that career proved highly enduring. How she explains her 1987 disco recording of 'Nellie The Elephant' is less cut and dried.

SONIC BOOM

'Boom Boom Boomerang' wasn't simply another attempt to maximize the *Boom!* effect for the Eurovision judges in 1977. The song was, in fact, intended to be a parody of the contest and the wider music industry. Austrian band **Schmetterlinge** presented possibly the most ridiculous performance yet seen in the contest, deliberately mimicking many previous entries. Nobody was particularly amused, although ironically perhaps, the song just avoided last place. That was achieved by Sweden's homage to the greatest pop band of all time, **The Beatles**.

THE BIG BANG

Monaco was the first to include *Boom* in a song when **Minouche Barelli** yelled 'Boum Badaboum' to an unsuspecting audience at the 1967 contest in Vienna. Though she managed only 5th place, other writers spotted that Minouche may have got something with **Serge Gainsbourg's** lyrics, even though it was a far inferior effort from his 1965 contest winner 'Poupée De Cire, Poupée De Son' ('Wax Doll, Singing Doll'), which had catapulted **France Gall** to fame and fortune. Something that was not achieved by Minouche.

In 1977, Schmetterlinge's ill-fated entry parodied Eurovision.

THE BOOM HAS LEFT THE ROOM

Having been away from the contest for over a decade, Denmark might be forgiven for not realizing that *Boom!* had become a by-word for bad Eurovision lyrics in the intervening years since their last appearance. That might explain why **Mabel's** 'Boom Boom' was sent to Paris in 1978 to mark their (less than) triumphant return. The French jury loved it, but nobody else was terribly impressed and **Mabel** sank to 16th place in the field of 20.

THE CHARM OFFENSIVE

Other Scandinavian hearts going Boom! followed and in 2000, Norwegian girl trio **Charmed** failed to charm the judges with 'My Heart Goes Boom'. Girl power was clearly not the order of the day for **Charmed**, although in fairness, their 11th place was the best Norway had achieved since finishing 2nd on home ground four years earlier.

BOOM BOOM

As relative newcomers to Eurovision, perhaps Armenians weren't aware that Denmark had failed miserably with 'Boom Boom' in 1978. Adding an exclamation mark to give it that distinctive edge, Armenia chose 'Boom Boom!' to go to Düsseldorf in 2011 with **Emmy** chosen to perform the song in the first semi-final. Armenia's record at Eurovision is pretty strong, there being only one entry to date that didn't reach the grand final – that failure being Emmy's 'Boom Boom!' Doubtless the Armenians won't be going *Boom!* again in the foreseeable future.

BOOM, BLAST AND RUIN

Luxembourg veered away from the repetitive Booms in 1971, but only marginally, substituting the fruity 'Pomme Pomme Pomme' ('Apple, Apple, Apple') in place of the explosive. **Monique Melsen** seemed cheerful enough on the stage in Dublin, but was probably happier when the trite wording was dropped for the English single release, becoming 'The Love Beat'. The rather embarrassing French lyric was surprisingly the result of a collaboration between two former Eurovision winning composers, **Hubert Giraud** and **Pierre Cour**. They probably should have quit whilst they were ahead.

In 2011 Emmy's hopes of reaching the final went Boom!

All Kinds Of Everything

UNEXPECTED ACTS

It takes a village and a broad church to build a world, but it takes a broad mind to sometimes understand all that's happening on the Eurovision stage. Over the years, there have been some pretty random sights that almost defy description, let alone categorization.

OVER THE TOP

Sweden's **Lasse Holm & Monica Törnell** didn't just go over the top with 'E' De' Det Här Du Kallar Kärlek' ('If It's This You're Calling Loving') in 1986. They soared so far over that they may still be up there somewhere, laughing. A skinny weightlifter, a fainting French maid, a man in a lavender bowler hat and the head of SVT's delegation bare-chested in leather trousers with a rock guitar would simply never be seen anywhere else but Eurovision. That they placed 5th with one of the stronger entries of the night says it all.

RAIDERS OF THE LOST ARK

Glam rock came to Sweden in 2007, possibly three decades after it went out of fashion elsewhere. **The Ark**'s 'The Worrying Kind' earned the country its worst result since 1992 – though it has scored even worse since. In the same contest, France's male **Les Fatal Picards**, resplendent in crushed velvet and feather boas, raced around the Helsinki stage singing lyrics that largely just *sounded* French. 'L'Amour À La Française' ('Love French Style') was really just individual – and stereotypical – French phrases with a heck of a lot of English thrown in. It was one of France's six entries to miss the Top 20.

Sweden's The Ark reinvented Glam Rock in 2007 – to no avail.

In 2008, Latvia's 'Wolves of the Sea' failed to impress.

DIVINE INSPIRATION

Spain and France both broke with tradition in 2008 and amused, baffled and outraged the audience into the bargain. **Sébastian Tellier** was already in trouble for having no French at all in his English song 'Divine'. Arriving on stage driving a golf-cart, while his five female backing singers all mimicked his appearance, replete with beards, **Sébastian** walked the stage barefoot in slow motion, carrying an inflatable globe. His bizarre staging was forgotten by the time Spain's **Rodolfo Chikilicuarte** with his Elvis quiff, robotic mannequin backers and miniature keyboard/saxophone arrived to perform 'Baila El Chiki Chiki' ('Dance The Chiki Chiki'). When asked for the inspiration for the song in his various press conferences, it's probably best not to repeat his reply. It's probably illegal even in Spain.

LOST AT SEA

Latvia's **Pirates Of The Sea** in 2008 brought hearty laughter and jolly rogering to Eurovision with 'Wolves Of The Sea'. Ireland's "douze points" helped them attain 12th place. Meanwhile, Ireland's glove puppet **Dustin The Turkey** was well and truly stuffed.

SHOCK TACTICS

Romania's **Cezar** turned in an operatic opus in Malmö 2013 with 'It's My Life' and a staging that amazed even the most jaded of the watching millions. He was dressed as a glittering vampire, and an unseen hydraulic lift allowed him to rise above his singers and dancers (clad only in their underwear), his black frock extending as he rose. Romania has qualified for every final since 2004 and clearly knows what the audience wants, even if they are left gaping-mouthed as they're given it.

IT'S A DRAG

Sometimes things work inexplicably, yet similarly off-beat ideas fall flat on their face. As drag queen **Verka Serduchka** shot up the scoreboard in 2007 with 'Dancing Lasha Tumbai', it may well have irked Denmark's own drag act **DQ**, who was packing his bags for home after being dumped out in the semi-final with 'Drama Queen'. His feathered headdress caused problems even on his way out because it simply couldn't fit in the backstage lifts at the Helsinki Arena.

La La La...

SONGS WITH "LA, LA LA" IN LYRICS

When in doubt, just sing "La, La, La"!
To a casual viewer, that could easily be
reasoned to be the fallback option for
endless Eurovision entrants.

The Duskeys' 'Here Today, Gone
Tomorrow' was prophetic in 1982.

LA LA LA IN LONDON

Although a recurring lyric substitute over the six
decades, only Spain's **Massiel** actually walked
off with the Grand Prix thanks to the absent of
any real lyric. 'La, La, La...' won out in London
1968, by simply repeating *La* 137 times. At the
culmination of the show, **Massiel** reprised the
song with the English lyric for the chorus. "He
Gives Me Love" were the English words, which
raised the question, why did the writers not take
the trouble to also compose words in Spanish?

NO JUMPING FOR JOY

1963 saw Germany trying the same tactic with
Heidi Brühls' 'Marcel'. Heidi took advantage
of the freedom of overhead boom microphones
to twirl her way around the set, but hadn't
taken the time to develop a stronger lyric. With
a quarter of the class of 63 failing to score at
all, her 5 points and 9th place were probably
something of a relief. The next German to try
the *La La* luck was Joy Fleming in 1975. Joy
was joyless at placing 17th of the 19 songs.

OOH LA LA LA!

The record for the most number of *La, La, La*s is, of course, held by Spain, but not by **Massiel**.
Betty Missiego's 'Su Canción' ('Your Song') actually recorded far more occurrences of the
banal filler. In fairness, Betty's own lyric had little in the way of *La*s but for her four child backing
singers, that was all they had to remember for three minutes. That and unfurling banners saying
"Thank you" in Spanish, Hebrew, English and French. 152 *La, La, La*s later, Spain had to wait in
agony to watch as their own jury handed victory to their Israeli rival.

IRE-LA-LA-LAND

Ireland's **Tina Reynolds** and **The Duskeys** didn't let their English language advantage get in the way of a good round of *La, La, La*. Tina's 'Cross Your Heart' and **The Duskeys'** 'Here Today, Gone Tomorrow' both avoided the need for a lyric with the Euro fallback in 1974 and 1982 respectively. For **The Duskeys**, 11th was Ireland's worst yet result for an English song. Only the country's single Gaelic entry, in 1972, fared worse. Tina reportedly had to write the lyrics on her hand in Brighton due to memory loss after an accident.

DO RE MI FA SO LA (LA) TI DO

Greece kicked off their Eurovision career in 1974 with a whole lot of *La*s in **Marinella**'s 'Krassi Thalassa Ke T'Agori Mou' ('Wine, Sea, My Boyfriend And Me'). Placing 11th with 7 points, Greece sat out the next edition and returned with a protest song in 1976. Wisely perhaps, the Greeks didn't try *La, La, La* again, but did get their best result prior to 2001 when in 1977, **Pascalis, Marianna, Robert & Bessy** gave 'A Music Lesson' for the viewers, repeatedly reciting the musical alphabet, Do Re Mi Fa So La Ti Do.

A TWIST ON A CLASSIC

The abolition of the native language rule in 1999 didn't see the end of the *La, La, La* standby unfortunately and as recently as 2012, Cyprus were still trying out the lyric, admittedly with a slight twist. 'La La Love' went to Baku with **Ivi Adamou** singing in English. She made the final, but couldn't make the voters fall in love with her *La La*s on the night. She placed 16th, yet remains her nation's last finalist to date.

Ivi Adamou's 'La La Love' was a minor hit in the UK.

A Little Peace

SONGS ABOUT PEACE AND LOVE

As in most pop music, the theme of love (shared, unrequited, passionate, broken, unwanted, etc.) has probably been Eurovision's most consistent theme over its 60-year history.

UNITED NATIONS

Ralph Siegel keeps returning to the theme of peace, love and harmony, his Swiss entry for 2006 being the most recent example. 'If We All Give A Little' was played out by **Six4One**, six singers from six different nations, hoping to demonstrate cross-border accord in Athens. The rest of Europe wasn't interested and they achieved a lukewarm 17th place, and the Swiss failed to qualify for the final again until 2012.

A QUEST FOR PEACE

German **Chris Kempers** teamed with Croatian **Daniel Kovac** to sing **Ralph Siegel** and **Michael Kunze's** peace offering 'Frie Zu Leben' ('Free To Live') in Zagreb, 1990. Of the songs keying into the theme of the night, Germany's offering was the most successful, but could still manage only 9th place.

THREE TIMES A HARM

One of only two songs in English to actually have the word "peace" in its title, Malta's 'Believe 'n' Peace' from **Times Three** in 1999 seemed a likely vote-catcher. Malta had after all, hit the Top 10 at every contest since their return from the wilderness in 1991 and indeed had climbed to a peak of 3rd the previous year in Birmingham. The three silver-clad ladies of the group believed they had the winner, yet the televoters weren't believing it at all. Placing 15th was the island nation's worst result from 1991 to 2000 and soon after **Times Three** went in three separate directions.

Multinational Six4One opened the 2006 contest for Switzerland with a German-composed song in English.

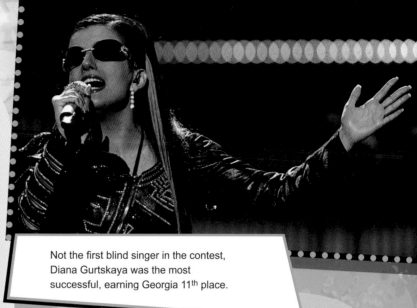

SEEING IS BELIEVING

Diana Gurtskaya was the blind singer performing Georgia's second Eurovision effort in 2008, hoping to improve on her country's debut 12th place from the year before. She did manage it, but 11th was hardly that impressive a move up the scoreboard. Although since 9th remains Georgia's high watermark, it's not bad. 'Peace Will Come' was impressive for the performance put together by Diana and her troupe of backing singers. All were dressed in black, and a giant sheet briefly descended and immersed the singers before the final chorus. Although invisible for just seconds, they emerged from beneath their shroud all in white. It was very impressive, but sadly, not enough to earn much goodwill from their continental brothers and sisters.

Not the first blind singer in the contest, Diana Gurtskaya was the most successful, earning Georgia 11th place.

EDGE OF A CLIFF

It's highly unlikely **Doug Flett** and **Guy Fletcher** had international harmony on their minds when they penned the UK's 1973 Eurovision entry 'Power To All Our Friends' for **Cliff Richard**. The lyric seems to be about deriving emotional power from valleys, wine, bees, sunshine and rock 'n' roll. However, revisionists like to point out that it could also be a sly dig by anti-Europeans: were the words a hidden metaphor protesting that Britain had joined the Common Market on January 1, 1973 and supporting those who felt the UK's power was transferring to their new European friends? Surely not.

A LITTLE PEACE

Peace and international harmony is most certainly a recurring lyric that has been tried over and over (and over) again. Only **Nicole**'s *'Ein Bißchen Frieden' (A Little Peace)* has actually triumphed with the theme of nation loving nation, but that's not deterred many others from giving it a go.

Flying The Flag

NATIONALISTIC AND GEOGRAPHICALLY MISPLACED ENTRIES

National pride and the urge to mark momentous events have influenced many entries over the years.

PATRIOT GAMES

Surprising, perhaps, to find one of Europe's landmark monuments included in the Eurovision encyclopedia, but 'Brandenburg Gate' was indeed the English title of Norway's entry to the 1990 contest in Zagreb. It was the year a large number of countries jumped on the theme of the momentous events of the previous autumn and the liberation of Eastern Europe from Soviet rule and the fall of the Iron Curtain; but like all the others, it failed to win over the more cynical jurors. Particularly so for **Ketil Stokkan**'s ode to the collapse of the Berlin Wall, which earned him last place, scoring just 5 points.

BIG MOUTH COMES FIFTH

Maggie MacNeal had been eclipsed by **ABBA** in 1974, so returned without her friend **Mouth** to try again on home ground in 1980. Although the contest was in Den Haag, Maggie sang about 'Amsterdam', which might have been confusing for anyone watching at home. Iinitially, it looked during the scoring like Maggie was going to run away with the victory, but in the end, she had to settle for 5th place.

VARIATIONS ON A THEME

Some themes do sometimes work and in Paris 1978, French duo **Caline & Olivier Toussaint** performed 'Les Jardins De Monaco' ('The Gardens of Monaco') for the Principality. The judges liked it, placing it 4th. They also liked **Alice & Franco Battiato's** local tribute 'I Treni Di Tozeur' ('The Trains Of Tozeur'), which scored 5th place in 1984. **Aud Wilken** tried something very different in 1995, singing of the Danish towns Mols and Skagen to a syncopated rhythm. 'Fra Mols Til Skagen' ('From Mols To Skagen') surprised many with 5th place.

COMPOSE YOURSELF

The same year **Maggie MacNeal** sang about Amsterdam, Austria sent a group of boys and girls to sing 'Du Bist Musik' ('You Are Music') under the name **Blue Danube**. The patriotically name combo's song was more or less a list of famous composers set to music: Chopin, Debussy, Liszt, Offenbach, Gershwin, Boulez, Strauss, Mahler, Schubert, Tchaikovsky, Puccini, Stravinsky and a host of others were name-checked. Surprising, really, that the song's composer didn't throw himself into the lyric.

In 2005, Martin Stenmarck crashed to 19th place, relegating his country into the semi-finals.

THE TIMES THEY ARE A CHANGIN'

In 1979, Austria tried to curry local favour with 'Heute In Jerusalem' ('Tonight In Jerusalem') by **Christina Simon**. Nobody likes a suck-up and Austria finished joint last. However, by 1999 attitudes had changed and back in Israel, to some **Sürpriz,** Germany's 'Reise Nach Jerusalem (Kudüs'e Seyahat)' ('Journey To Jerusalem') swept up the scoreboard to 3rd. There's just no telling.

NOT QUITE UNITED STATES

America proved fatal for The Netherlands in 1979 when 'Colorado' was the theme of **Xandra**'s Dutch entry, placing 14th. Luxembourg tried the theme again in 1981, bringing back former winner **Jean-Claude Pascal** to croon 'C'est Peut-être Pas L'Amérique' ('Maybe It's Not America'). He didn't do too badly, placing 11th, but Norway reaching out back across the Atlantic to 'San Francisco' in 1997 earned them their record-breaking fourth "nul points". More recently, Sweden was sent packing with **Martin Stenmarck**'s 'Las Vegas' in 2005.

HELLO FROM MARS, GOODBYE FROM EUROVISION

Singing about local places or even far flung places is clearly risky. Leaving the Earth altogether is certainly a very bad idea. On home ground, a year after their win with **Marie N**, Latvian group **F.L.Y.** went into orbit to say 'Hello From Mars' and slumped into the bottom 3. Germany's 'Planet Of Blue' in 1996 failed to reach the final, breaking Germany's record of having appeared in every Eurovision final.

Marija Naumova scored Latvia's first win in just three attempts with 'I Wanna' in 2002.

115

Hard Rock Hallelujah

EUROVISION ROCK ACTS

Although specifically created to promote "popular music" Eurovision has embraced a wide range of musical styles in its 60-year history. Although "pop" has generally found the most success, everything from opera to death metal has been tried.

SOME KIND OF MONSTER

Death metal monster rockers **Lordi**'s *'Hard Rock Hallelujah'* may have been the most extreme music style to win in 2006, but in fact, the style of the monster rockers' presentation masked a fairly routine pop song underneath.

Teräsbetoni tried but failed to equal the success of their fellow rockers Lordi.

MY SWEET LORDI?

Having won with a rock metal sound, Finland had another stab at the genre in 2008, when rock group **Teräsbetoni** went to Belgrade with 'Missä Miehet Ratsastaa' ('Where The Men Ride'). They made the final, but ended 22nd in the results. Suggestions that the band may have been **Lordi** without their grotesque costumes and masks were swiftly denied by Finnish TV and the bands themselves, but has anyone ever see the two groups together?

THE FIRST ROCK

Norway's glam rock band **Wig Wam** can largely be credited as having entered Eurovision's first rock song when 'In My Dreams' won through to the 50th anniversary contest in 2005, electrifying the audience in Kyiv and topping the Norwegian singles chart. The flamboyant performance from the spandex and fur-clad rockers may have overwhelmed the song itself, ending Norway's pattern of winning the contest in year's ending in "5" begun by **Bobbysocks** 20 years earlier.

Norway's Wig Wam brought Glam Metal Rock to Eurovision 2005.

THIS COWBOY SONG

Country and Western is another rare musical genre to find its way into Eurovision and hasn't proved particularly successful when tried. The two most obvious examples are Austria's debut in 1957 'Wohin, Kleines Pony?' ('Where To, Little Pony?') from **Bob Martin**, which placed last and Germany's 'No No Never' in 2006. **Texas Lightning** were highly tipped to carry off the win in Athens and came to Greece already No. 1 at home and climbing the Austrian and Swiss charts. The bands's 14th place came as something of a shock to the fans and certainly a surprise to the group. Nonetheless, the track ended the year as the second biggest-selling single in Germany.

Arja, Hannu, Seppo, Harry, Kim & Hendrik combined as Pihasoittajat in 1975.

IT'S NOT UNUSUAL

It might not be possible to categorize Finland's 'Viulu-Ukko' ('Old Man Fiddle') from **Pihasoittajat** as country music, as it was more a hybrid of folk, hillbilly pop and country. Certainly the most unusual rhythm Finland had sent to Eurovision to date in 1975, the song also got them fiddling up to 7th, a near best result.

THE SOPRANOS

Opera is another genre not particularly at ease with the Eurovision judges, albeit when it's applied more as light operetta. Stage star (but never a hit maker) **Patricia Bredin** got the UK off to a very shaky start in 1957 with her soprano rendition of 'All' placing 7th of the 10 entries. 'Nur In Der Wiener Luft' ('Only In The Viennese Air'), sung by **Eleonore Schwarz** in 1962, was an operatic tour de force, but unfortunately the song had nothing whatsoever to do with current popular music. Eleonore's operatic opus was a consummate performance, but opera failed to fit in to the world of "pop" music and was always bound to be passed over by the judges. Dressed in a crinoline, she certainly was the performer of the night, but it was an experiment destined for failure and "nul points".

Lordi, Finland's sole Eurovision winner, performing in 2006.

Absent Friends

COUNTRIES THAT HAVE NEEDED A EUROVISION BREAK FROM TIME TO TIME

It was the United Kingdom who became Eurovision's first nation to withdraw from the contest, and a number of others have decided to take breaks from the competition, only to return to the fold fairly soon after.

RECORD BREAKERS

Having failed to register in time for the inaugural contest in 1956, Britain's debut entry came in Frankfurt the following year. Such was the British public's lack of interest in their operatic song 'All' that their chosen representative **Patricia Bredin** didn't even bother to record it. Ms. Bredin was also at odds with the song's musical director, **Eric Robinson**, who waved the baton before his artist was even in place. Thankfully for Patricia, it was the shortest song ever performed in the contest's history, so her agony was not prolonged. With such a weak result and poor viewing figures, the British didn't show up the following year, but returned in 1959 to begin a record-setting 57-year streak of continuous entries.

POOR SCORES

Luxembourg followed in the UK's footsteps by skipping the 1959 competition, but like their Anglo competitor clearly regretted the decision and returned in 1960 for the first contest staged in London. The following year, they kickstarted a hugely successful run of five wins in 32 years, before withdrawing after being relegated from the 1994 contest due to poor scores. Despite annual rumours to the contrary, the Grand Duchy has refused to enter ever since.

DENMARK LEAVES A MARK

Denmark triumphed in the eighth Eurovision Song Contest, having been present since the second. Clearly of the opinion there was nothing left for them to achieve, they made 1966 their last appearance for over a decade. Thankfully, a new broom arrived at Danmarks Radio in 1977 and the following year, the Danes returned to the competition, scoring two wins in the years since and steadfastly remaining the only Scandinavian nation never to have failed to score.

Katie Boyle checks the running order with Denmark's Katy Bødtger in 1960.

EUROVISION SONG CON
1 UNITED KIN
2 SWEDEN
3 LUXEMBOU
4 DENMARK
5 BELGIUM
6 NORWAY
7 AUSTRIA
8 MONACO
9 SWITZERLA
10 HOLLAND
11 GERMANY
12 ITALY
13 FRANCE

When Massiel won in 1968, Cliff Richard joked of shaking her warmly by the throat.

A TRIUMPHANT RETURN

Austria objected to the contest being staged under Franco's fascist regime in 1969, so stayed away from the Madrid competition, despite their single point for Spain in 1968 being partly responsible for the unexpected Spanish win in the first place. The ensuing fracas over the four-way tie meant Austria also boycotted the 1970 edition in Amsterdam. They returned for 1971 and 1972. Having failed to qualify in both 2005 and 2007 (they didn't enter at all in 2006), Austrian TV took a break and a rethink until 2011. The break did them good. Although they didn't make the 2013 final, they returned in triumph in 2014.

INDEPENDENT NATIONS

Yugoslavia's break-up was followed by the disintegration of the Soviet Union. In many parts of Eastern Europe, the fledgling independent nations all lined up eagerly to join the Eurovision Song Contest. For some, it was easier than others and Slovakia have remained absent from the Eurovision final since 1998, although after a decade away, they did at least enter the semi-finals four times from 2009 to 2012, without progressing to the show's climax.

MOROCCO AND CO.

Monaco stepped off the Eurovision stage after **Laurent Vaguener** secured their second worst result ever in 1979 and are yet to return to the final, but their place was taken in the 1980 line-up by Morocco. The Moroccans made this a one-off attempt to integrate with their European cousins and have avoided the ensuing 35 contests completely.

LONGEST ABSENCES FROM THE CONTEST

MONACO~ (Last appeared in 1979 final)	35 years
MOROCCO* (Last appeared in 1980 final)	34
YUGOSLAVIA ^ (Last appeared in 1992 final)	22
LUXEMBOURG (Last appeared in 1993 final)	21
MALTA (Absent 1976–1990)	16
SLOVAKIA~ (Last appeared in 1998 final)	16
ITALY (Absent 1998–2010)	13
DENMARK (Absent 1967–1977)	11

* ONLY ONE ENTRY.
^ NO LONGER EXISTS AS A NATION. ALL FORMER YUGOSLAV CONSTITUENTS HAVE ENTERED THE CONTEST INDEPENDENTLY.
~ HAS ENTERED THE SEMI-FINALS BUT FAILED TO QUALIFY.

ANDORRA GIVES UP!

Andorra never made it to the Eurovision final, despite six attempts from various European nationalities. After failing at the semi-final stage yet again in 2009, the tiny mountainous enclave has opted to give the contest a wide berth.

After finishing 3rd in 1973, Sweden's ABBA returned to triumph in *Melodifestivalen 1974*, going on to score their nation's first ever Eurovision win in Brighton with 'Waterloo' and changing Eurovision forevermore.

## CHAPTER FIVE

Records

After 60 years, there is a wealth of fascinating statistics
detailing everything you need to know about which European
nations can call themselves champions and – more importantly
– what nations need to Bucks Fizz their ideas up.

Most Successful Songs By Nation

Based on each result and relative score, which songs have proved the most successful for each of Eurovision's 51 competing nations?

AUSTRIA

1.	Rise Like A Phoenix	Conchita Wurst	1st 2014
2.	Merci Chérie	Udo Jürgens	1st 1966
3.	Sag Ihr Ich Lass Sie Grüßen	Udo Jürgens	4th 1965
4.	Falter Im Wind	The Milestones	5th 1972
5.	My Little World	Waterloo & Robinson	5th 1976
6.	Nur Ein Lied	Thomas Forstner	5th 1989
7.	Die Ganze Welt Braucht Liebe	Liane Augustin	=5th 1958
8.	Weil Der Mensch Zählt	Alf Poier	6th 2003
9.	Warum, Nur Warum?	Udo Jürgens	6th 1964
10.	Du Hast Mich So Fasziniert	Harry Winter	7th 1960

BELGIUM*

1.	J'Aime La Vie	Sandra Kim	1st 1986
2.	Sanomi	Urban Trad	2nd 2003
3.	L'Amour Ça Fait Chanter La Vie	Jean Vallée	2nd 1978
4.	Si Tu Aimes Ma Musique	Stella	4th 1982
5.	Un Peu De Poivre, Un Peu De Sel	Tonia	=4th 1966
6.	Avanti La Vie	Jacques Zegers	=5th 1984
7.	Ma Petite Chatte	Fud Leclerc	=5th 1958
8.	Dis Oui	Mélanie Cohl	6th 1998
9.	Me And My Guitar	Tom Dice	6th 2010
10.	Mon Amour Pour Toi	Fud Leclerc	6th 1960

*Excludes the 1956 contest

BOSNIA-HERZEGOVINA

1.	Lejla	Hari Mata Hari	3rd 2006
2.	Love In Rewind	Dino Merlin	6th 2012
3.	Putnici	Dino & Beatrice	7th 1999
4.	In The Disco	Deen	9th 2004
5.	Bistra Voda	Regina	9th 2009
6.	Pokušaj	Laka	10th 2008
7.	Rijeka Bez Imena	Maria Šestić	11th 2007
8.	Na Jastuku Za Dvoje	Maja Tatić	=13th 2002
9.	Call Me	Feminem	14th 2005
10.	Hano	Nino Pršeš	14th 2000

CROATIA

1.	Marija Magdalena	Doris Dragović	4th 1999
2.	Sveta Ljubav	Maja Blagdan	4th 1996
3.	Neka Mi Ne Svane	Danijela	5th 1998
4.	Nostalgija	Magazin & Lidija	6th 1995
5.	Kada Zaspu Andeli (Ostani)	Goran Karan	9th 2000
6.	The Strings Of My Heart	Vanna	10th 2001
7.	Vukovi Umiro Sami	Boris Novković feat. Lado Members	11th 2005
8.	Everything I Want	Vesna Pisarović	11th 2002
9.	Moja Štikla	Severina	13th 2006
10.	You Are The Only One	Ivan Mikulić	13th 2004

CYPRUS

1.	Mono I Agapi	Anna Vissi	5th 1982
2.	Stronger Every Minute	Lisa Andreas	5th 2004
3.	Mana Mou	Hara & Andres Constantinou	5th 1997
4.	Gimme	One	6th 2002
5.	Monica	Island	6th 1981
6.	Aspro Mavro	Alexia Vassiliou	7th 1987
7.	Sti Fotia	Alexandros Panayi	9th 1995
8.	Mono Gia Mas	Constantinos	9th 1996
9.	S.O.S.	Elena Patroclou	9th 1991
10.	Teriazoume	Evridiki	11th 1992

DENMARK

1.	Fly On The Wings Of Love	The Olsen Brothers	1st 2000
2.	Only Teardrops	Emmelie De Forest	1st 2013
3.	Dansevise	Grethe & Jørgen Ingmann	1st 1963
4.	Never Ever Let You Go	Rollo & King	2nd 2001
5.	Vi Maler Byen Rød	Birthe Kjær	3rd 1989
6.	Ka' Du Se Hva' Jeg Sa?	Hot Eyes	3rd 1988
7.	Skibet Skal Sejle I Nat	Birthe Wilke & Gustav Winckler	3rd 1957
8.	Det' Lige Det	Hot Eyes	4th 1984
9.	In A Moment Like This	Chanée & N'evergreen	4th 2010
10.	Fra Mols Til Skagen	Aud Wilken	5th 1995

ESTONIA

1.	Everybody	Tanel Padar, Dave Benton & 2XL	1st 2001
2.	Runaway	Sahlene	=3rd 2002
3.	Once In A Lifetime	Ines	4th 2000
4.	Kaelakee Hääl	Ivo Linna & Maarja-Liis Ilus	5th 1996
5.	Diamond Of Night	Evelin Samuel & Camille	6th 1999
6.	Rändajad	Urban Symphony	6th 2009
7.	Kuula	Ott Lepland	6th 2012
8.	Keelatud Maa	Maarja-Liis Ilus	8th 1997
9.	Mere Lapsed	Koit Toome	12th 1998
10.	Et Uus Saaks Alguse	Birgit Õigemeel	20th 2013

FINLAND

1.	Hard Rock Hallelujah	Lordi	1st 2006
2.	Tom Tom Tom	Marion Rung	6th 1973
3.	Viulu-Ukko (Old Man Fiddle)	Pihasoittajat	7th 1975
4.	Laiskotellen	Lasse Mårtenson	7th 1964
5.	Tipi-Tii	Marion Rung	=7th 1962
6.	Tie Uuteen Päivään	Markku Aro & Koivisto Sisters	8th 1971
7.	Eläköön Elämä	Sonja Lumme	9th 1985
8.	Hengaillaan	Kirka	9th 1984
9.	Lapponia	Monica Aspelund	10th 1977
10.	Playboy	Ann Christine Nystroem	=10th 1966

FRANCE*

1.	L'Oiseau Et L'Enfant	Marie Myriam	1st 1977
2.	Un Premier Amour	Isabelle Aubret	1st 1962
3.	Dors Mon Amour	André Claveau	1st 1958
4.	Tom Pillibi	Jacqueline Boyer	1st 1960
5.	Un Jour Un Enfant	Frida Boccara	=1st 1969
6.	Un, Deux, Trois	Catherine Ferry	2nd 1976
7.	C'Est La Dernier, Qui A Parlé, Qui A Raison	Amina	2nd 1991
8.	White And Black Blues	Joelle Ursull	=2nd 1990
9.	La Belle Amour	Paule Desjardins	2nd 1957
10.	Humanahum	Jean Gabilou	3rd 1981

*Excludes the 1956 contest

GERMANY*

1.	Ein Bißchen Frieden	Nicole	1st 1982
2.	Satellite	Lena Meyer-Landrut	1st 2010
3.	Theater	Katja Ebstein	2nd 1980
4.	Johnny Blue	Lena Valaitis	2nd 1981
5.	Lass Die Sonne In Dein Herz	Wind	2nd 1987
6.	Für Alle	Wind	2nd 1985
7.	Nur Die Liebe Läßt Uns Leben	Mary Roos	3rd 1972
8.	Diese Welt	Katja Ebstein	3rd 1971
9.	Reise Nach Jerusalem (Kudüs'e Seyahat)	Sürpriz	3rd 1999
10.	Wir Geben 'Ne Party	Mekado	3rd 1994

*Excludes the 1956 contest

GREECE

1.	My Number One	Helena Paparizou	1st 2005
2.	Shake It	Sakis Rouvas	3rd 2004
3.	Die For You	Antique	3rd 2001
4.	Secret Combination	Kalomira	3rd 2008
5.	Mathema Solfege	Pascalis, Marianna, Robert & Bessy	5th 1977
6.	Olou Tou Kosmou I Elpida	Cleopatra	5th 1992
7.	Alcohol Is Free	Koza Mostra Feat. Agathon Iakovidis	6th 2013
8.	Yassou Maria	Sarbel	7th 2007
9.	Watch My Dance	Loucas Yiorkis Feat. Stereo Mike	7th 2011
10.	This Is Our Night	Sakis Rouvas	7th 2009

HUNGARY

1.	Kinek Mondjam El Vétkeimet	Frederika Bayer	4th 1994
2.	Running	András Kállay-Saunders	5th 2014
3.	Unsubstantial Blues	Magdi Rúzsa	9th 2007
4.	Kedvesem (Zoohacker Remix)	ByeAlex	10th 2013
5.	Forogj, Világ	Nox	12th 2005
6.	What About My Dreams?	Kati Wolf	22nd 2012
7.	Új Név A Régi Ház Falán	Csaba Szigeti	22nd 1995
8.	A Holnap Már Nem Lesz Szomorú	Charlie	23rd 1998
9.	Sound Of Our Hearts	Compact Disco	24th 2012
10.	Árva Reggel	Andrea Szulák	SF 1993

ICELAND

1.	All Out Of Luck	Selma	2nd 1999
2.	Is It True?	Yohanna	2nd 2009
3.	Eitt Lat Enn	Stjórnin	4th 1990
4.	Nei Eða Já	Heart 2 Heart	7th 1992
5.	Nætur	Sigga	12th 1994
6.	Tell Me!	Einar Agust Vidisson & Telma Agustdottir	12th 2000
7.	Sjúbidú	Anna Mjöll Olafsdottir	13th 1996
8.	Þá Veistur Svarið	Inga	13th 1993
9.	This Is My Life	Euroband	14th 2008
10.	No Prejudice	Pollapönk	15th 2014

IRELAND

1.	All Kinds Of Everything	Dana	1st 1970
2.	Rock & Roll Kids	Paul Harrington & Charlie McGettigan	1st 1994
3.	Hold Me Now	Johnny Logan	1st 1987
4.	What's Another Year?	Johnny Logan	1st 1980
5.	In Your Eyes	Niamh Kavanagh	1st 1993
6.	The Voice	Eimear Quinn	1st 1996
7.	Why Me?	Linda Martin	1st 1992
8.	Terminal Three	Linda Martin	2nd 1984
9.	If I Could Choose	Sean Dunphy	2nd 1967
10.	Somewhere In Europe	Liam Reilly	=2nd 1990

ISRAEL

1.	A-Ba-Ni-Bi	Izhar Cohen & Alpha Beta	1st 1978
2.	Diva	Dana International	1st 1998
3.	Hallelujah	Milk & Honey with Gali Atari	1st 1979
4.	Hi	Ofra Haza	2nd 1983
5.	Hora	Avi Toledano	2nd 1982
6.	Kaan	Duo Datz	3rd 1991
7.	Ey-Sham	Ilanit	3rd 1973
8.	Hasheket Shenishar	Shiri Maimon	4th 2005
9.	Olé Olé	Izhar Cohen	5th 1985
10.	Emor Shalom	Chocolate Menta Mastik	6th 1976

ITALY*

1.	Non Ho L'Età	Gigliola Cinquetti	1st 1964
2.	Insieme: 1992	Toto Cutugno	1st 1990
3.	Madness Of Love	Raphael Gualazzi	2nd 2012
4.	Si	Gigliola Cinquetti	2nd 1974
5.	Era	Wess & Dori Ghezzi	3rd 1975
6.	Uno Per Tutte	Emilio Pericoli	3rd 1963
7.	Gente Di Mare	Umberto Tozzi & Raf	3rd 1987
8.	Nel Blu Di Pinto Di Blu	Domenico Modugno	3rd 1958
9.	Rapsodia	Mia Martini	3rd 1992
10.	Fiumi Di Parole	Jalisse	4th 1997

*Excludes the 1956 contest

LATVIA

#	Song	Artist	Place/Year
1.	I Wanna	Marie N	1st 2002
2.	My Star	Brainstorm	3rd 2000
3.	The War Is Not Over	Walters & Kazha	5th 2005
4.	Wolves Of The Sea	Pirates Of The Sea	12th 2008
5.	Questa Notte	Bonaparti.lv	16th 2007
6.	I Hear Your Heart	Cosmos	16th 2006
7.	Too Much	Arnis Mednis	=18th 2001
8.	Hello From Mars	F.L.Y.	24th 2003
9.	Cake To Bake	Aarzemnieki	SF 13th 2014
10.	Beautiful Song	Anmary	SF 16th 2012

LITHUANIA

#	Song	Artist	Place/Year
1.	We Are The Winners	LT United	6th 2006
2.	You Got Style	Skamp	13th 2001
3.	Love Is Blind	Donny Montell	14th 2012
4.	C'Est Ma Vie	Evelina Sašenko	19th 2011
5.	Strazdas	Aiste	20th 1999
6.	Love Or Leave	The 4Fun	21st 2007
7.	Something	Andrius Pojavis	22nd 2013
8.	Happy You	Aivaras	23rd 2002
9.	Love	Sasha Son	24th 2009
10.	Lopšinė Mylimai	Ovidijus Vyšniauskas	25th 1994

LUXEMBOURG*

#	Song	Artist	Place/Year
1.	Tu Te Reconnaîtras	Anne-Marie David	1st 1973
2.	Après Toi	Vicky Leandros	1st 1972
3.	Si La Vie Est Cadeau	Corinne Hermès	1st 1983
4.	Poupée De Cire, Poupée De Son	France Gall	1st 1965
5.	Nous Les Amoureux	Jean-Claude Pascal	1st 1961
6.	L'Amour De Ma Vie	Sherisse Laurence	3rd 1986
7.	Petit Bonhomme	Camillo Felgen	3rd 1962
8.	Croire	Lara Fabian	3rd 1988
9.	Dès Que Le Printemps Revient	Hugues Aufray	=4th 1964
10.	L'Amour Est Bleu	Vicky Leandros	4th 1967

*Excludes the 1956 contest

MALTA

#	Song	Artist	Place/Year
1.	7th Wonder	Ira Losco	2nd 2002
2.	Angel	Chiara	2nd 2000
3.	The One That I Love	Chiara	3rd 1998
4.	Little Child	Mary Spiteri	3rd 1992
5.	More Than Love	Moira & Chris	5th 1994
6.	Could It Be?	Paul Giordimaina & Georgina	6th 1991
7.	Desire	Claudette Pace	8th 2000
8.	Tomorrow	Gianluca	8th 2013
9.	This Time	William Mangion	8th 1993
10.	Let Me Fly	Debbie Sceri	9th 1997

MONACO

#	Song	Artist	Place/Year
1.	Un Banc, Un Arbre, Une Rue	Séverine	1st 1971
2.	Dis Rien	François Deguelt	2nd 1962
3.	Toi, La Musique Et Moi	Mary Christy	3rd 1976
4.	Où Sont-Elle Passées?	Romuald	3rd 1964
5.	Ce Soir Là	François Deguelt	3rd 1960
6.	Une Petite Français	Michèle Torr	4th 1977
7.	Les Jardins Des Monaco	Caline & Olivier Toussaint	4th 1978
8.	Celui Qui Reste Et Celui Qui S'En Va	Romuald	=4th 1974
9.	L'Amour S'En Va	Françoise Hardy	=5th 1963
10.	Boum-Badaboum	Minouche Barelli	5th 1967

THE NETHERLANDS*

#	Song	Artist	Place/Year
1.	Ding Dinge Dong	Teach-In	1st 1975
2.	Net Als Toen	Corry Brokken	1st 1957
3.	Een Beetje	Teddie Scholten	1st 1959
4.	De Troubadour	Kenny Kuhr	=1st 1969
5.	Calm After The Storm	The Common Linnets	2nd 2014
6.	I See A Star	Mouth & MacNeal	3rd 1974
7.	Als Het Om De Liefde Gaat	Sandra & Andres	4th 1972
8.	Hemel En Aarde	Edsilia Rombley	4th 1998
9.	Amsterdam	Maggie MacNeal	5th 1980
10.	Rechtop In De Wind	Marcha	=5th 1997

*Excludes the 1956 contest

NORWAY

#	Song	Artist	Place/Year
1.	Fairytale	Alexander Rybak	1st 2009
2.	La Det Swinge	Bobbysocks	1st 1985
3.	Nocturne	Secret Garden	1st 1995
4.	I Evighet	Elizabeth Andreassen	2nd 1996
5.	Intet Er Nytt Under Solen	Åse Kleveland	3rd 1966
6.	I'm Not Afraid To Move On	Jostein Hasselgård	4th 2003
7.	I Feed You My Love	Margaret Berger	4th 2013
8.	Voi Voi	Nora Brockstedt	=4th 1960
9.	Alle Mine Tankar	Silje Vige	5th 1993
10.	For Vår Joord	Karoline Krüger	5th 1988

POLAND

#	Song	Artist	Place/Year
1.	To Nie Ja!	Edyta Górniak	2nd 1994
2.	Keiner Grenzen – Żadnych Granich	Ich Troje	7th 2003
3.	Ale Jestem	Anna-Maria Jopek	11th 1997
4.	My Slowianie – We Are Slavic	Donatan & Cleo	14th 2014
5.	Chcę Znać Swój Grzech	Kasia Kowalska	15th 1996
6.	To Takie Proste	Sixteen	17th 1998
7.	Love Song	Blue Café	17th 2004
8.	Przytul Mnie Mocno	Mietek Szcześniak	18th 1999
9.	Sama	Justyna	18th 1995
10.	2 Long	Piasek	20th 2001

PORTUGAL

#	Song	Artist	Place/Year
1.	O Meu Coração Não Tem Cor	Lúcia Moniz	6th 1996
2.	A Festa Da Vida	Carlos Mendes	7th 1972
3.	Um Grande, Grande Amor	José Cid	7th 1980
4.	Chamar A Música	Sara Tavares	8th 1994
5.	Lusitana Paixão	Dulce	8th 1991
6.	Menina	Tonicha	9th 1971
7.	Sobe Sobe Balão Sobe	Manuela Bravo	9th 1979
8.	Tourada	Fernando Toro	=10th 1973
9.	A Cicade Até Ser Dia	Anabella	10th 1993
10.	Silêncio E Tanta Gente	Maria Guinot	11th 1984

ROMANIA

#	Song	Artist	Place/Year
1.	Playing With Fire	Paula Seling & Ovi	3rd 2010
2.	Let Me Try	Luminita Anghel & Sistem	3rd 2005
3.	Tornerò	Mihai Trăistariu	4th 2006
4.	Tell Me Why	Monica Anghel & Marcel Pavel	9th 2002
5.	Don't Break My Heart	Nicola	10th 2003
6.	Miracle	Paula Seling & Ovi	12th 2014
7.	Zaleilah	Mandinga	12th 2012
8.	Liubi, Liubi, I Love You	Todomondo	13th 2007
9.	It's My Life	Cezar	13th 2013
10.	Change	Hotel FM	17th 2011

RUSSIA

#			
1.	Believe	Dima Bilan	1st 2008
2.	Solo	Alsou	2nd 2000
3.	Never Let You Go	Dima Bilan	2nd 2006
4.	Party For Everybody	Buranovskiye Babushki	2nd 2012
5.	Ne Verj, Ne Bojsia, Ne Prosi	t.A.T.u.	3rd 2003
6.	Song #1	Serebro	3rd 2006
7.	What If We?	Dina Garipova	5th 2013
8.	Shine	Tolmachevy Sisters	7th 2014
9.	Vechni Stranik	Youddiph	9th 1994
10.	Northern Girl	Premier Ministr	10th 2003

SERBIA˜ - SERBIA & MONTENEGRO˄ - MONTENEGRO*

#			
1.	Molitva	Marija Šerifović	1st 2007~
2.	Lane Moje	Željko Joksimović	2nd 2004^
3.	Nije Ljubav Stvar	Željko Joksimović	3rd 2012~
4.	Oro	Jelena Tomašević feat. Bora Dugic	6th 2008~
5.	Zauvijek Moja	No Name	7th 2005^
6.	Ove Je Balkan	Milan Stanković	13th 2010~
7.	Čaroban	Nina	14th 2011~
8.	Moj Svijet	Sergej Ćetković	19th 2014*
9.	Cipela	Marko Kon & Milaan Nikolić	SF 10th 2009~
10.	Get Out Of My Life	Andrea Demirović	SF 11th 2009*

SLOVENIA

#			
1.	Prisluhni Mi	Darja Švajger	7th 1995
2.	Energy	Nusa Derenda	7th 2001
3.	Zbudi Se	Tanja Ribič	10th 1997
4.	For A Thousand Years	Darja Švajger	11th 1999
5.	No One	Maja Keuc	13th 2011
6.	Samo Lujbezen	Sestre	=13th 2002
7.	Cvet Z Juga	Alenka Gotar	15th 2007
8.	Naj Bogovi Slišijo	Vili Resnik	18th 1998
9.	Dan Najlepših Sanj	Regina	21st 1996
10.	Tih Deževan Dan	1x Band	=22nd 1993

SPAIN

#			
1.	La, La, La…	Massiel	1st 1968
2.	Vivo Cantando	Salomé	=1st 1969
3.	Eres Tú	Mocedades	2nd 1973
4.	En Un Mundo Nuevo	Karina	2nd 1971
5.	Su Canción	Betty Missiego	2nd 1979
6.	Vuelve Conmigo	Anabel Conde	2nd 1995
7.	Lady, Lady	Bravo	3rd 1984
8.	Bailar Pegados	Sergio Dalma	4th 1991
9.	Gwendolyne	Julio Iglesias	=4th 1970
10.	Bandido	Azúcar Moreno	5th 1990

SWEDEN

#			
1.	Euphoria	Loreen	1st 2012
2.	Diggi-Loo, Diggi-Ley	Herreys	1st 1984
3.	Take Me To Your Heaven	Charlotte Nilsson	1st 1999
4.	Fångad Av En Stormvind	Carola	1st 1991
5.	Waterloo	ABBA	1st 1974
6.	Nygammal Vals Eller Hip Man Svinaherde	Lill Lindfors & Svante Thuresson	2nd 1966
7.	Främling	Carola	3rd 1983
8.	Undo	Sanne Nielsen	3rd 2013
9.	Bra Vibrationer	Kikki Danielsen	3rd 1985
10.	Popular	Eric Saade	3rd 2011

SWITZERLAND*

#			
1.	Ne Partez Pas Sans Moi	Céline Dion	1st 1988
2.	Refrains	Lys Assia	1st 1956
3.	Pas Pour Moi	Daniela Simons	2nd 1986
4.	T'En Va Pas	Esther Ofarim	2nd 1963
5.	Giorgio	Lys Assia	2nd 1958
6.	Moi Tout Simplement	Annie Cotton	3rd 1993
7.	Amour On T'Aime	Arlette Zola	3rd 1982
8.	Nous Avrons Demain	Franca Di Rienzo	3rd 1961
9.	Io Senza Te	Peter, Sue and Marc	4th 1981
10.	Cinema	Paola Del Medico	4th 1980

*Excludes one of Switzerland's results from the 1956 contest

TURKEY

#			
1.	Everyway That I Can	Sertab Erener	1st 2003
2.	We Could Be The Same	maNga	2nd 2010
3.	Dinle	Şebnem Paker & Group Etnic	3rd 1997
4.	For Real	Athena	4th 2004
5.	Düm Tek Tek	Hadise	4th 2009
6.	Shake It Up Shekerim	Kenan Doğulu	4th 2007
7.	Deli	Mor Ve Ötesi	7th 2008
8.	Love Me Back	Can Bonomo	7th 2012
9.	Halley	Klips Ve Onlar	9th 1986
10.	Yorgunum Anla	Pinar Ayhan & SOS	10th 2000

UKRAINE

#			
1.	Wild Dances	Rulsana	1st 2004
2.	Dancing Lasha Tumbai	Verka Serduchka	2nd 2007
3.	Shady Lady	Ani Lorak	2nd 2008
4.	Gravity	Zlata Ognevich	3rd 2013
5.	Angel	Mika Newton	4th 2011
6.	Tick-Tock	Mariya Yaremchuk	6th 2014
7.	Show Me Your Love	Tina Karol	7th 2006
8.	Sweet People	Alyosha	10th 2010
9.	Be My Valentine (Anti Crisis Girl)	Svetlana Loboda	12th 2009
10.	Hasta La Vista	Olexsandr	14th 2003

UNITED KINGDOM

#			
1.	Save Your Kisses For Me	Brotherhood Of Man	1st 1976
2.	Puppet On A String	Sandie Shaw	1st 1967
3.	Love Shine A Light	Katrina & The Waves	1st 1997
4.	Making Your Mind Up	Bucks Fizz	1st 1981
5.	Boom Bang-A-Bang	Lulu	=1st 1969
6.	Beg, Steal Or Borrow	The New Seekers	2nd 1972
7.	Let Me Be The One	The Shadows	2nd 1975
8.	Rock Bottom	Lynsey de Paul & Mike Moran	2nd 1977
9.	Where Are You?	Imaani	2nd 1998
10.	Better The Devil You Know	Sonia	2nd 1993

YUGOSLAVIA

#			
1.	Rock Me	Riva	1st 1989
2.	Džuli	Danijel	4th 1983
3.	Ja Sam Za Ples	Novi Fossili	4th 1987
4.	Ne Pali Svetlo U Sumrak	Lola Novaković	=4th 1962
5.	Mangup	Srebrna Krila	6th 1988
6.	Hajde De Ludujemo	Tajči	7th 1990
7.	Brez Besed	Berta Ambrož	=7th 1966
8.	Jedan Dan	Luci Kapurso & Hamo Hajdarhodzić	=7th 1968
9.	Neke Davne Sveta	Ljiljana Petrović	8th 1961
10.	Vse Rože Sveta	Lado Leskovar	=8th 1967

ALBANIA

1.	Suus	Rona Nishlu	5th 2012
2.	The Image Of You	Anjeza Shahini	7th 2004
3.	It's All About You	Juliana Pasha	16th 2010
4.	Tomorrow I Go	Ledina Celo	16th 2005
5.	Zemrën E Lamë Peng	Olta Boka	17th 2008

ARMENIA

1.	Not Alone	Aram MP3	4th 2014
2.	Qele Qele	Sirusho	4th 2008
3.	Apricot Stone	Eva Rivas	7th 2010
4.	Without Your Love	André	8th 2006
5.	Anytime You Need	Hayko	8th 2007

AZERBAIJAN

1.	Running Scared	Ell/Nikki	1st 2011
2.	Hold Me	Farid Mammadov	2nd 2013
3.	Always	AySel & Arash	3rd 2009
4.	When The Music Dies	Sabina Babyeva	4th 2012
5.	Drip Drop	Safura	5th 2010

BELARUS

1.	Work Your Magic	Koldun	6th 2007
2.	Solayoh	Alyona Lanskaya	16th 2013
3.	Cheesecake	Teo	16th 2014
4.	Butterflies	2+1 Feat. Robert Wells	24th 2010
5.	Eyes That Never Lie	Petr Elfimov	SF 13th 2009

Former Yugoslav Republic of MACEDONIA

1.	Ninanajna	Elena Risteska	12th 2006
2.	Crno I Bela	Kaliopi	13th 2012
3.	Mojot Svet (My World)	Karolina	14th 2007
4.	Life	Toše Proeski	14th 2004
5.	Make My Day	Martin Vučić	17th 2005

GEORGIA

1.	Shine	Sofia Nizharadze	9th 2010
2.	One More Day	Eldrine	9th 2011
3.	Peace Will Come	Diana Gurtskaya	11th 2008
4.	Visionary Dream	Sopho	12th 2007
5.	Waterfall	Sophie & Nodi	15th 2013

MOLDOVA

1.	Boonika Bate Doba	Zdob Şi Zdub	6th 2005
2.	Fight	Natalia Barbu	10th 2007
3.	Lăutar	Pasha Parfeny	11th 2012
4.	O Mie	Aliona Moon	11th 2013
5.	So Lucky	Zdob Şi Zdub	12th 2011

SLOVAKIA

1.	Kým Nás Maš	Marcel Palonder	18th 1996
2.	Nekonečná Pieseň	Martin Durinda & Tublatanka	=19th 1994
3.	Modlitba	Katerina Hasprová	21st 1998
4.	I'm Still Alive	Twiins	SF 12th 2011
5.	Horehronie	Kristína Peláková	SF 16th 2010

THE BEST OF THE REST

1. Water	Elitsa Todorova & Stoyan Yankoulov	Bulgaria	5th 2007
2. Bitakat Hob	Samira Bensaid	Morocco	18th 1980
3. Maybe	Valentina Monetta	San Marino	24th 2014
4. Salvem El Món (Let's Save The World)	Anonymous	Andorra	SF 12th 2007
5. Have Some Fun	Tereza Kerndlová	Czech Republic	SF 18th 2008
6. Quand Tout S'Enfuit	Aline Lahoud	Lebanon	Withdrawn 2005
7. No Entry Chosen	No Singer Chosen	Tunisia	Withdrawn 1977
8. Little Cowboy	Biggi Bachman	Liechtenstein	Possibly 1976*

see page 99

Overall Records

The Eurovision Song Contest may be a friendly competition but it is a competition! Find out which countries and languages lead the way.

WINNERS' TABLE

IRELAND	7	70, 80, 87, 92, 93, 94, 96	MONACO	1	71
LUXEMBOURG	5	61, 65, 72, 73, 83	BELGIUM	1	86
FRANCE	5	58, 60, 62, 69*, 77	YUGOSLAVIA	1	89
UNITED KINGDOM	5	67, 69*, 76, 81, 97	ESTONIA	1	01
SWEDEN	5	74, 84, 91, 99, 12	LATVIA	1	02
THE NETHERLANDS	4	57, 59, 69*, 75	TURKEY	1	03
ISRAEL	3	78, 79, 98	UKRAINE	1	04
NORWAY	3	85, 95, 09	GREECE	1	05
DENMARK	3	63, 00, 13	FINLAND	1	06
SWITZERLAND	2	56, 88	SERBIA	1	07
ITALY	2	64, 90	RUSSIA	1	08
AUSTRIA	2	66, 14	AZERBAIJAN	1	11
GERMANY	2	82, 10			
SPAIN	2	68, 69*			

* Shared victory

WINNING LANGUAGES

ENGLISH	28	67, 69*, 70, 74–76, 80–81, 87, 92–94, 96–97, 99–03, 05–06, 08–14
FRENCH	14	56, 58, 60–62, 65, 69*, 71–73, 77, 83, 86, 88
DUTCH	3	57, 59, 69*
HEBREW	3	78, 79, 98
SPANISH	2	68, 69*
GERMAN	2	66, 82
SWEDISH	2	84, 91
ITALIAN	2	64, 90
NORWEGIAN	2	85, 95
SERBO CROAT	2	89, 07
DANISH	1	63
ENGLISH/UKRAINIAN	1	04

* Shared win

WINNING PERFORMERS BY TYPE OF ARTIST

Ignoring uncredited backing performers

FEMALE SOLOISTS∞	37	56–57, 59–60, 62, 64–65, 67–68, 69 (x 4), 70–73, 77, 82–83, 86, 88, 91–93, 96, 98–99, 02–05, 07, 10, 12–14
MALE/FEMALE GROUPS	10	74, 75, 76, 78, 79, 81, 89, 95, 97, 06
MALE SOLOISTS*	8	58, 61, 66, 80, 87, 90, 08, 09
MALE DUOS	3	94, 00, 01
MALE/FEMALE DUOS	2	63, 11
MALE GROUPS	1	84
FEMALE DUOS	1	85

∞ Includes 2014 winner, male drag artist Conchita Wurst.

*Includes two wins for Johnny Logan.

WINNING COMBOS (Counting all performers on stage)

ONE PERFORMER	12	56, 58, 59, 60, 61, 62, 64, 65, 66, 69 (FRANCE), 70, 14
TWO PERFORMERS	5	57, 63, 69 (THE NETHERLANDS), 94, 12*
THREE PERFORMERS	1	69 (UNITED KINGDOM)
FOUR PERFORMERS	8	67, 68, 69 (SPAIN), 76, 79, 81, 87, 93
FIVE PERFORMERS	12	71, 72, 80, 86, 88, 89, 95, 96, 98, 03, 08, 10
SIX PERFORMERS	22	73–75, 77–78, 82–85, 90–92, 97, 99–02, 04–07, 09, 11, 13

*Sweden's backing singers in 2012 were off-stage.

THE LONG AND THE SHORT OF IT! (FINALS ONLY)

LONGEST CONTEST:	MALMÖ 2013	3 hours, 30 minutes
LONGEST PERFORMANCE:	ITALY 1957	'Corde Della Mia Chitarra' (5:09)
LONGEST SONG TITLE:	GERMANY 1964	'Man Gewöhnt Sich So Schnell An Das Schöne'
LONGEST ARTIST NAMES		
GROUP:	LUXEMBOURG 1985	MARGO, FRANCK OLIVIER, CHRIS ROBERTS, MALCOLM ROBERTS, IREEN SHEER & DIANE SOLOMON
SOLOIST:	ICELAND 1987	HALLA MARGRÉT ANADOTTIR*
SHORTEST CONTEST:	FRANKFURT 1957	1 hour, 9 minutes
SHORTEST PERFORMANCE:	UNITED KINGDOM 1957	'All' (1:52)
SHORTEST SONG TITLES:	ITALY 1974	'Si'
	SPAIN 1982	'El'
	ISRAEL 1983	'Hi'
	UNITED KINGDOM 1988	'Go'
SHORTEST ARTIST NAMES		
GROUPS:	ICELAND 1986	ICY
	TURKEY 1985 & 1988	MFÖ~
	TURKEY 1989	PAN
	CROATIA 1993	PUT
	HUNGARY 1997	VIP
	CROATIA 1997	ENI
	FYR MACEDONIA 2000	XXL
	PORTUGAL 2001	MTM
	CYPRUS 2002	ONE
	LATVIA 2003	F.L.Y.
	HUNGARY 2005	NOX
SOLOISTS:	GERMANY 2003	LOU
	GERMANY 2004	MAX
	BELARUS 2014	TEO

The shortest named contestants ever were 2B, who failed to qualify for Portugal in 2005; and DQ, who didn't qualify for Denmark in 2007.

3JS failed to qualify for the 2011 final representing the Netherlands and PeR failed to qualify for the 2013 final representing Latvia.

*The longest named solo artist would have been Jóhanna Guðrún Jónsdóttir, representing Iceland in 2009, but she opted for the stage name Yohanna for her performance.

~Also referred to as Mazhar, Fuat & Özkan